Don't Need the Sunshine

JOHN OSBORNE

For my grandmas

Published by AA Publishing, a trading name of AA Media Limited,
Fanum House, Basing View, Basingstoke, Hampshire, RG21 4EA, UK.
Registered number 06112600.

First published in 2013

A CIP catalogue record for this book is available from the
British Library.

ISBN: 978-0-7495-7397-3

A04795

Design and layout: Tracey Butler

Proofreader: Joey Clarke

Printed and bound in the UK by Clays Ltd

www.theAA.com

Our books carrying the FSC label are printed on FSC certified paper.
FSC is the only forest certification scheme endorsed by the leading
environmental organisations.

CONTENTS

PART FOUR: WEST

ABOUT THE AUTHOR

John Osborne is a writer and broadcaster based in Norwich. His first book, *Radio Head*, was broadcast as Radio 4's *Book of the Week*. He has had poetry published in the *Guardian*, *The Big Issue* and the *Spectator* and his first full collection of poetry, *Most People Aren't That Happy, Anyway*, was published in 2013. He is a regular performer at festivals including Latitude, Glastonbury and Bestival. He is the writer and performer of three Radio 4 shows: *John Peel's Shed*, *The Newsagent's Window* and *Valentine's Day*. His debut solo show, *John Peel's Shed*, enjoyed a sell-out run at the Edinburgh Fringe in 2011. *Don't Need the Sunshine* is his third book.

www.johnosbornewriter.com

Foreword

It's six months since I finished writing my book and I'm at the seaside again. It's New Year's Day and I'm in a café in Felixstowe. I've spent so much of my life visiting seaside resorts, reading and writing about them, and they continue to dominate my conversations.

When I started writing my book everyone I spoke to had suggestions for me. 'You have to go to ...' they would say, inserting a town of their choice because it's the best or worst, saddest or most mediocre seaside you could ever visit. People have such strong associations with the seaside. I'd spent a year collecting the stories of people who have lived and worked by the seaside. I wanted to ask the questions I've always wanted answering. Is it possible to walk away with a profit on those 2p machines in the arcades? Did the romance of the seaside die with the birth of Ryanair? What is the future of our seaside towns?

It has been physically impossible to visit all the seaside towns recommended to me. Practically every beach in the

UK has been mentioned at some stage. This is a book about those I have managed to visit, the towns whose cafés, pubs and museums I have spent time at, whose benches I've sat on to admire the views. At home the wall by my desk is covered with postcards of the places I have been to. Skegness, Hastings, Blackpool. Rude postcards bought at the saucy postcard museum I visited on the Isle of Wight. Souvenirs of a year spent with sand in my shoes. I made connections with my past. Traced family footsteps. Went to seaside resorts I'd been to hundreds of times before as well as ones I didn't know existed.

Felixstowe is one of the towns I didn't originally have the chance to visit, despite being urged to do so. 'Check out the Cliff Top Tea Rooms by the seafront,' I'd been instructed. At a loose end on New Year's Day, this is where I ended up.

The Cliff Top Tea Rooms are a place where people look out at the sea while squeezing the life out of a teabag, refilling the pot with hot water. Here the world moves at the speed of the rotating cake stand displaying Victoria sponge, apple strudel, lemon cheesecake, scones. The café is crowded, the sound of polite chatter audible. Most people, I imagine, are reminiscing. There is little else to do in January at the seaside.

The café was suggested to me because there is something special about it: you have that feeling you are in a bygone age. Everything about the café, from the tablecloths to the politeness of the staff as they brought pots of tea, is traditional and quaint. A sign advertises freshly cut sandwiches. It feels like we're all waiting for a steam train.

The feeling I have in this café is one that I have felt so many times at the seaside: a feeling of safety in nostalgia.

The bad things can't reach us here. There are many negative associations with the British seaside, but I have tried to focus on places like this.

As has so often been the case over the previous months I find myself surrounded by contented people. On the table next to me is a group of four, their bicycles chained to the railings outside, their woolly gloves and fluorescent jackets stuffed inside their cycle helmets. They read the ice cream menu to each other: 'Amarena cherry sundae. Vanilla ice cream topped with Fragola strawberries, meringue and fresh whipped cream.' At the serving hatch, by the rack of Twinings tea bags and tub of Tutti Frutti lollipops, is a laminated sign: *If you want breakfast in bed sleep in the kitchen.* The waitress brings my scone, clotted cream and strawberry jam. It felt rude not to order one.

Outside, people walk along the seafront. The sea and fresh air don't close down for a Bank Holiday. Three generations sit on a bench dedicated to a fourth. Two little girls ride bikes with stabilisers. A couple enjoy their New Year's Day hand-in-hand walks. They spent last night watching Jools Holland's *Hootenanny* and looked out the window this morning, thinking, 'It's a lovely day, let's go to the seaside.' Beyond the beach, the sea sparkles; a sight I will never get bored of.

In writing this book I've stumbled across stories of romance, family histories going back generations, and new ideas to make our seaside prosperous. I've met a retired lighthouse keeper, dozens of Mr Punches, and the lady who organises the UK sandcastle building competition. I've learned about the history and future of the seaside; met bed and breakfast owners, artists, and those campaigning to restore theatres and lidos and Winter Gardens to their previous glories.

The British seaside has never failed to inspire me, and I hope you will be equally inspired by the people and places in this book.

John Osborne
On the train back to Norwich, New Year's Day 2013

Part One
NORTH

CHAPTER ONE

Beacock Family Cricket

On my desk I have a photograph taken on Scarborough Beach on 7 August 1990. I know it was then because my dad writes the date on the back of every photograph he takes. The picture is of me and my sister, my mum and dad, all suntanned and smiling in our shorts and hats. I've had it in its frame in every house I've lived in: halls of residence, university houses and beyond, always there on my desk, next to the stapler I never use and my mug that says *John* which I keep my pens in. An image of somewhere familiar and comforting.

Scarborough was somewhere we visited regularly when I was growing up. My sister sometimes suffered with travel sickness, and my dad knew that anywhere further than an hour's drive would jeopardise the upholstery of his Volkswagen Polo. Rather than trekking too far we'd head for the Yorkshire coast: usually Scarborough, or occasionally to

Whitby or Robin Hood's Bay. I'd always be so excited, pack my cricket bat and ball in the boot, feel the weight of my summer pocket money in my Velcro wallet as we headed to the beach.

I used to go on long walks along the beach. Not just any walk: epic adventures. I walked and walked, my trousers rolled up to my knees as the waves crashed at my feet; all the things that were scrambled up in my adolescent head seemed to gain reassuring clarity by the sea. My mum, dad and sister would waste their time doing things like reading and relaxing. Sometimes I would join them, lie down in the sun. My sister and I would lie next to each other, sharing a pair of headphones, one ear each, listening to the latest *Now That's What I Call Music* tape we'd bought in January using our Christmas Our Price vouchers. Most of the time I'd walk up and down the seafront, putting the world to rights in my head.

When we were a little bit older we started to go to France on our holidays. My mum was a French teacher and we wouldn't be allowed to have an ice cream unless we asked for it ourselves in French. I've never been keen to talk to a stranger at the best of times, not even if the reward was a mint choc chip. But despite the good weather and the benefits towards our French GCSE speaking exam, I always preferred it when we holidayed closer to home.

To be honest, the idea of a couple of weeks somewhere hot has never really appealed to me. In the summer after my first year of university, the rest of my housemates went for a week-long binge, being lads on sunloungers somewhere sunny. I stayed at home. 'What if I can never re-create this happiness?' I always think as soon as a good thing happens. Maybe I was worried that if it was too nice there I wouldn't be able to recover when I got back. I just liked it where I was. I've often wondered if there is really such a need to travel for hours at huge cost and stress when you can just travel a few miles to your nearest seaside town. When you're having a break, it doesn't matter how close or far away you are from your everyday life. The important part is the unwinding. You don't have to go to the other side of the world to do that.

The seaside dominates our family photo albums. Christmas and summer holidays on the beach were the two times in the year we were most likely to hear the words 'Let's get the camera out.' These photographs captured that different side of ourselves we experienced at the seaside. Being at the seaside gave us a chance to re-create ourselves, to escape our day to day lives. Even now, a mention of the sea is enough to lift my spirits and fill me with a sense of joyful optimism. That's one of the reasons I have that family photograph from Scarborough Beach on my desk. It's also one of the reasons I decided to write this book.

The idea to write about the seaside came to me when I found myself returning to Scarborough for work. I'd got a job at a summer school and it felt odd to be back there, returning to the resort. The last time I'd been to Scarborough was when my sister and I were 18, the day before our A-level results.

Our dad could see we were both worried so he told us to pack a bag for the beach, then drove us to Scarborough to take our mind off it. His plan worked perfectly, until we got in the car to go home.

'See,' he said. 'You've not even thought about your A-level results, have you?'

Karen and I spent the rest of the journey panicking and stressed, looking out of the window, the Yorkshire countryside disappearing behind us as we contemplated our grim futures.

Several years after those results, I was back in town, this time to earn a living. The teaching was hard work, but being back in Scarborough more than made up for it. Once the course had finished, I had a day to myself before I had to catch the train home. It was time to retrace my teenage steps and go on one of those adventures along the beach I'd always enjoyed as a child.

I set off down the high street from the bed and breakfast where I'd been staying. The road leading down to South Bay Beach had so many shops selling sticks of rock, buckets and spades and other memorabilia. The seaside trades on this – nostalgia and chips. I passed two joke shops selling pots of slime, fake blood and Osama Bin Laden masks. There were shops selling plastic swords and also a mug shop: slogans on enamel included *The World's Greatest Piss Artist, World's Greatest Lazy Bastard* and *The World's Greatest Shagger.* Strictly speaking, I think you need to be awarded these things rather than buy them yourself.

Next door to the mug emporium was a novelty T-shirt shop. *I'm not bald, it's a solar panel for a sex machine. Instant idiot: just add alcohol. If found, please return to pub.* It was tempting to despair, but I caught sight of a couple of wool shops at that moment; no innuendo here, just knitting needles, balls of wool and cotton reels. Perhaps there was something left of the old Scarborough after all.

'Where's granddad gone?' a little girl with her hair in bunches asked her mum.

The whole family looked around. 'Where's he gone?'

No-one knew. He's always wandering off, that granddad.

'Where's granddad gone?' they repeated, starting to get slightly anxious. Outside a charity shop a grey-haired man was checking his Nokia.

I came to Arrow Models, a shop that brought back a thousand tiny happy memories: Meccano, Scalextric, dumper trucks, little trains, model aircrafts, toy cars ... I could remember every square inch of carpet in that shop. It was as much a part of our holiday as the beach or the fish and chips. There were beads for making jewellery, microscopes, practical jokes, massive jigsaw puzzles, card games, model boats, junior tool kits, tubes of glue, doll's house furniture, doll's house wallpaper, painting by numbers, Eeyores and Piglets. It was a shop whose stock ends up in Christmas stockings across Yorkshire.

As I walked down to the front, the faded glamour of the Grand Hotel came into view. It was built in 1863 – among the first large, purpose built hotels in Europe – and was immediately in high demand as an unprecedented number of visitors arrived in the area, drawn by the newly fashionable pastime of sea bathing. Seawater was believed to cure illnesses and this was the reason Scarborough had first developed as a resort. It was even suggested that drinking the seawater could cure gout. There must have been a lot of it about, because Scarborough started attracting more visitors than the town could accommodate, hence the building of the Grand. No expense was spared in its facilities: the original plumbing even gave guests the option to choose between seawater or fresh water.

In recent years, though, the Grand Hotel had suffered a series of misfortunes. Once one of the most luxurious places to stay in the country, it had now become a budget hotel. Changes of management and bad press due to unfortunate outbreaks of illness amongst guests did not help, not to mention the shift to people going abroad on their holidays, rather than to seaside resorts like Scarborough.

I couldn't resist taking a look inside. In the corner was a *Viz* quiz machine, at the opposite side of the room an unplayed grand piano. Despite its declining fortunes, there was still a bustle to the Grand's dining room. It still felt like a special place to sit, whether for a cream tea or an Apple and Mango J20.

By now, I could smell the whiff of the sea air. It was time to start thinking about putting my socks and shoes into my rucksack and rolling up my trouser legs as I made my way down to the seafront. A local radio station was blaring out from a car stereo. No doubt the DJ had a baseball cap on and his top off in the studio. He was about to explode with excitement, eulogising the weather as he played a remix of *The Sun is Shining* by Bob Marley. I walked to the beachside café to buy a bottle of water. It was too hot for Coca-Cola; this was Solero and Evian weather. The whole of Britain was in the mood for a Lemon Sparkle.

Across Scarborough beach that week sunbathers had been applying their factor 25. It was approaching 30 degrees in the early afternoon, a proper school holidays scorcher. I remembered how those six weeks had always felt infinite, a month and a half with practically nothing to do. I was surprised to see such bright sunshine marking the summer break. When I was at school, there was torrential rain every single day of the holidays. Kids, they have it so much easier now.

As soon as my bare feet touched the sand, all my anxieties and problems were forgotten, and I could just walk. I was comforted by the seashells, the people shuffling along the beach hovering their metal detectors inches above the sand, the Wall's ice cream logo rotating in the breeze. A man was sat reading the new Alan Hollinghurst novel. I bet he'd saved that for his deckchair. 'I'll treat myself to this for the seaside,' he'd have said, patting its front cover in Waterstone's, taking it to the till.

Further along the beach, two boys were digging a massive hole. It's a little known fact, but if you dig deep enough, you get to Australia. Another group of kids were carrying buckets full of shells. If you hold a shell to your ear, sometimes you can hear a Beatles song playing backwards. A little boy and girl were burying their dad in the sand. He didn't look entirely willing to take part, but was letting them do it anyway. On his deckchair lay the newspaper he'd much rather have been reading.

Two boys were play-fighting. It was starting to get a little too violent. 'This will end in tears,' I thought, walking on. All over the beach in block capitals was the name Kylie. There was a big love heart, too, within it the words 'Scott loves Hannah 4eva'. We'll see about that in 20 years, Scott and Hannah. Someone had drawn a smiley face in the sand. I think it might have been Banksy.

I walked from one end of the beach to the other, just as I had done all those years ago. There were kids playing in the rock pools. These were essentially glorified puddles but nevertheless an army of youngsters paraded with their fishing nets, hoping for sight of a crab. There are few things more exciting as a child than exploring the rock pools. Hoping you'd maybe find a starfish, or be able to put something wiggling into your bucket.

Sitting cross-legged on the shoreline, close to the crashing of the waves, was a man staring out at the sea. That's what I love about the seaside. It's a place to have big thoughts. 'Why did I leave my wife?' he was thinking. Or perhaps, 'I am so happy right now and have come here to take stock of that.' Maybe he was just having a bit of quiet time before he had to do his chores: pick his daughter up from a friend's house, take them to Brownies.

A dog on a lead was being led into the sea by its overzealous owner, a little girl with pigtails. She was oblivious to his anxieties about the waves. 'I would really rather not,' the dog explained, in perfect English, but she didn't hear, too excited about the proximity of splashing. Beaches and real ale pubs

– the two best places to see good dogs. It's not just the dogs who are let off the leash at the seaside. Mums and dads are given licence not to be so parental. Strict mum and strict dad can become holiday mum and holiday dad.

I walked past a couple holding hands. What better place to be in love than the seaside? Love and lust aren't restricted to Hollywood rom-coms and *Hollyoaks* blondes. The beach is for everyone: a play area, somewhere to snooze, think, read, hula hoop, walk dogs, cuddle up, build sculptures, swim, and propose. There were teenagers in love, people who had been married for 30 years were in love. 'Oh yeah, we're in love,' they remember, taking each other's hands as they walk along the beach.

So many parents were messing around with their kids. 'They're not so bad after all,' they'd decided, leaving squabbles about homework and bathtime locked up in their homes, a key left with next door with instructions to water their plants. There was a really-good-at-football dad in his replica 1966 England shirt and three-quarter-length trousers doing tricksy back heels. He knew his kids would be impressed by him as he showboated with step-overs and dribbles and dinks – 'Our dad's the best at football.' Families never really get to see each other these days. But that changes when we're on holiday. A holiday at the seaside.

Too often summer is a forgotten season. It's the end of June, the sun comes out, you allow yourself to have a yawn, a stretch, and suddenly the 'Back to School' signs are up in BhS and Ryman and it turns out it's September again. You missed it and forgot to SkyPlus it. But right now, this was the seaside in summer.

I watched a family playing cricket. Let's call them the Beacocks. They were playing on the damp sand left by the retreating tide, the part of the beach where you get a more even bounce of a tennis ball. The dad bowled his left arm finger spin, remembering his days as a promising 20-year-old when he once almost had a trial with Warwickshire.

The boy batting hit the ball hard, and his fielding sister ran towards the horizon to retrieve it. As she did so, their mum took the opportunity to call out to another little boy, sitting by himself back at the deckchairs. I hadn't noticed him at first, but now Mrs Beacock was shouting 'Michael, Michael', waving for him to join them. As soon as he heard her calling, the boy jumped up and ran towards the game as fast as he could. He was waving with both hands and beaming a smile. Overjoyed at the reunion, he took his place in the field next to his wicket-keeping brother.

I think he might have been naughty. Maybe he'd done something bad earlier in the day and as a punishment the stricter of his parents would have said, 'For that, you can't play Beacock family cricket later.' Possibly he was sulking, had dropped his ice cream or had a headache or sunburn. Maybe he just didn't like cricket. He preferred to sit by himself and read a comic. But he hadn't realised that this wasn't about the cricket: it was about the Beacocks. He could read his comic any time, but Beacock family cricket only happened a couple of times a year. That was why his mum was worried about him, sitting there all by himself. He had served his punishment for earlier misdemeanours, and now it was time to join in. He was the best in the family at catching.

The game started again. The ball went straight past Michael, who was delighted to run and retrieve it. He threw the tennis ball back to his mum. The Beacock family were reunited. Everything was back to normal.

There have been generations of beach cricketers just like the Beacocks. In Michael Parkinson's autobiography he reminisces about going on holiday growing up: the first thing his dad would do when they got to the beach was to work out the best place to put the stumps. As the game started, his dad would invite others to join in, and these new-found friends would often return on the following days of their holiday.

In my family, I was the only one who ever wanted to play cricket. Unless there was a wall to keep me company I would wriggle impatiently all afternoon until the sun went in. It was the Scarborough Cricket Festival that gave me my first proper glimpse of cricket when I was about ten. The Festival had been going since 1876 – it was to have started a year earlier, but, as has been the perennial problem with English cricket, it was cancelled due to rain – and I couldn't really have chosen a better place to fall in love with the game.

The match I went to see was Yorkshire versus the 'Rest of the World'. My dad brought a copy of the rules along and explained to me as the game progressed what was happening, why the umpires and players were doing what they were doing. For most of the day I didn't have a clue what was going on, but still I loved every second; the announcer, the clapping, the chatter around me. Most cricket grounds in the UK are wonderful places, where life takes on a different meaning and the chatter of strangers can quickly turn into conversation with new friends, but the ground at Scarborough, with such history and sense of occasion, will always be very special to me.

I'm pretty sure Michael Beacock is going to be a famous cricketer when he grows up and he too will remember fondly those innings he played on Scarborough Beach. If in ten or fifteen years there's a promising blond fellow coming on for his England debut at Trent Bridge, that might well be Michael Beacock. Remember where you first heard that name. Although I did make it up, so don't hold your breath.

After spending time on the beach, reading, wandering and staring at people, I walked to the other side of town to visit Peasholm Park: woodland, gardens, ice cream stalls, a bandstand and a boating lake. This is where we always went when we were little. There were many things we loved about Scarborough but nothing more than Peasholm Park. Afternoons on the boating lake would always be a highlight of the summer: they have pedalos there!

As with so much associated with the British seaside, Peasholm Park suffered serious decline in the 1980s and 90s. In 1999, the pagoda was set on fire by vandals and there hasn't been money to restore it since. Even so, for many this remains a place of romance. Take the 1960s story of young love I found on the Peasholm Park website. In August 1965, Winnie and Tom sat next to each other on the coach on a Christian group trip to Peasholm Park. She was 25, Tom was 23. They didn't know each other, but talked briefly before going their separate ways. Later, Tom was walking by the lake on his own when it started raining. A group of girls called out to him, asking if he wanted to share their umbrella. Tom realised the girl holding the umbrella was the girl he had sat next to earlier on the coach. He reminded Winnie of that as she sheltered him from the rain. Seven months later they were married, and the couple spent 42 years together.

Revisiting the park in 2009, Tom told the website, 'for my late wife and for me, Peasholm Park was not just two words, but words that changed our lives forever.' I, too, hadn't expected to feel so moved being back at Peasholm Park. I remembered vividly the dragon boats, the waterfalls, bunting, rowing boats and ducks. There were so many kids with their parents and grandparents, it really put it into context what my sister and I must have looked like running around as children. There were little girls pushing pink pushchairs, people walking dogs, old people carrying coats over their arms, their jumpers tied over their shoulders. People were having so much fun, just as we had.

A sign at the park café offered 'Ice cream. Any flavour. £1.' That's just how life should work, I thought to myself. So often we try and make things too complicated. That's one of the things I love about the seaside. There remains something reassuring and familiar and relaxed about it.

I felt I had been missing out on something. Perhaps it was just nostalgia, but being at the seaside for the week had made me think. Peasholm Park, the sand in my shoes, the shop that sold the dumper truck – it turned out that my memory had bookmarked all these things.

I took out my phone, pulled up a map and scanned the coastline. I realised that despite such happy memories of being in Scarborough, 20 years on I'd been to very few British seaside resorts. I'd never been as far as Brighton, let alone Eastbourne, Bournemouth or Cornwall. As a child, you are told that when colouring in you should go all the way to the edges. I decided that maybe I should apply this to my travelling.

I had an idea. Why not spend a year travelling around the British seaside? Instead of going on a fortnight's holiday to somewhere with Cos in its name, I could go on day trips and weekends to seaside resorts instead. I could learn about their history and their future, meet the people who lived and worked there, collect their stories. I would spend more time walking along beaches, in the rain, the sun, and maybe even snow. I'd begin in the North East, in Redcar where my mum went on holiday as a child. Then I'd travel down the east coast, around East Anglia to Essex and the South. I'd follow the coast down to Cornwall, before heading back up to Blackpool and Morecambe via Wales.

So many people I knew were heading abroad, and not just on holiday. My best friend had recently moved to Australia, my sister now lived in Switzerland. I had itchy feet, too, but decided that rather than seeking the tropics or the continent, like the 19th-century crowds flocking to Scarborough, my cure would be the British seaside.

By the time I got back to South Bay, it was still sunny but the beach had started to empty. There was a different atmosphere completely; the mood had changed from matinee performance to evening show. A group of kids were smoking outside the ice cream café. The bins were overflowing after a day of indulgence by the day trippers: there were bottles and rubbish everywhere, and seagulls were making unsettling squawks and pecking at the KFC packaging.

I retraced my footsteps from earlier, but this time I was walking across a graveyard for trodden-on sandcastles. There was a trainer footprint on one squashed tower. Bits of seaweed sticking to a moat. Perfectly good sandcastles abandoned as the whole of the beach went to get their tea. There were only a few stragglers left, still making the most of being at the seaside. One couple unwrapped sandwiches from cling film. A group of girls shook out their blankets, washed sand from between their toes and put their jumpers over their sunburnt backs, packed their books back in their bags as they made plans for the evening. Hidden away by the wall another couple were kissing, really going for it, hands everywhere. They were old enough to know better. Maybe it was his birthday.

I looked at my watch; it was time to catch my train. I took one last look at the beach, and watched as a man carried his little boy, fast asleep, over his shoulder. The end of a long day at the beach. I, though, didn't feel tired. In fact I felt more awake, more energised than I had been for weeks, and had lots of ideas in my head. Scarborough had left me invigorated, and had reawakened my love for the seaside. It felt far too long since I had last been at the sea, but now I was ready to make up for lost time.

CHAPTER TWO

Last Train to Redcar

I decided to start my tour of seasides by going up to Redcar with my mum. She's from Teeside, and Redcar is where she used to go on day trips with her family as a little girl.

Redcar is not somewhere I remember as well or as fondly as Scarborough, but it was near my grandma's house so we'd go there sometimes. Sometimes we'd go a few miles further along to Saltburn-by-the-Sea. I remember my grandma once telling me the story of two old ladies there who owned a pet lion. They would take it for walks on the beach, locals were used to them. 'It's just the two old ladies with their lion,' they'd say. I never knew whether the story was true or not but I've always believed it. The rule of urban legends, I've decided, is that they are all true. Life is too short not to believe these stories.

My mum lived a few miles down the road from Redcar, or, more accurately, down the track. The area is famous for trains, most notably for its associations with the Stockton and Darlington Railway on which the world's first passenger train ran in 1825. Unsurprisingly, it used to be a real tourist hotspot too. When the Middlesbrough to Redcar railway opened in 1846, Redcar became a regular destination for Victorian tourists coming for their holidays.

Just like the Victorians, my mum and I were also travelling to Redcar by train. I've always felt a strong association with the railway, maybe because my granddad used to work on the trains. There's something about the heaps of coal by the tracks, men in 'high-vis' jackets shovelling. I still find myself counting the carriages when waiting in the car at the level crossing. I like it when I see trainspotters on the bridge with their notebooks, bobble hats, and the perfect vantage point. There's something reassuring about the cargo train disappearing over the horizon, its locomotive rhythms like a good story being told.

'It used to be such a treat to go to the seaside for an ice cream,' my mum remembered on the journey northwards. She reminded me of a café called Pacitto's that she used to go to when she was little, which we had decided to track down on our visit. Not that the weather ever seemed particularly suited to ice creams.

'If it was raining you'd just put a mac in your bag,' my mum told me, 'and spend the afternoon sheltering under a bandstand before getting the train back home. They were our days out.'

As she told me this, drizzle started to appear on the train window. It looked like being another rainy day at the seaside.

It's because of the railways that people first started holidaying at the seaside nearly 200 years ago. It was the space that attracted people; the coastline, fresh air, nature. Locals panicked, as you do when you get unexpected visitors at Christmas. We'd better get them something to eat, where are we going to put them? What are we going to do with them? Better get some extra chairs out. Trains grew to be so popular that the platforms and stations were dangerous places to be at times. In *Family Britain* by David Kynaston there's a report from Newcastle on the hottest day of the year in 1950, a day which a ticket collector described as 'pandemonium'.

Kynaston describes the scenes as 'a vivid moving mosaic of blues and reds and yellows and greens', as people were desperate to get to the seaside. It wasn't just the train networks that struggled to cope with the demand, it was also the resorts and local attractions, resulting in queues everywhere: 'Tyneside queued to enjoy itself. It queued for jugs of water, for countless picnic teas, it queued for lemonade and candyfloss; it queued to get on the beach, it queued to get off the beach.'

The seaside was heavily marketed by the train companies. Most famous was the friendly face of Sunny South Sam, a cheerful man in uniform tipping his cap. Sam was created by the Southern Railway, who described him as 'the helpful member of staff waiting to help you on arrival at an unknown location'. He first appeared in 1930 with a succession of cheerful slogans: *Buy British sunshine holidays* suggested one poster with Sunny South Sam, whose cheerful demeanour was the polar opposite of the General Kitchener one a few years earlier, pointing at anyone who came into his line of vision.

Sunny shores and cooling breezes, Southern Coastline always pleases, Sam continued. He really wanted people to have a lovely holiday. It's what he lived for. Sam and the Southern Railway claimed they could take you to the places that each year topped the 'sunshine league table'. At the time, the motor car was a toy for the rich and the best way of getting to the seaside was to go by train. Sunny South Sam did for seaside resorts in the south of England what Captain Birdseye has done for fish fingers.

Sam's reign only lasted as long as the outbreak of the Second World War, when the posters of sunshine and optimism were replaced by government ones telling people to keep calm and carry on. It wasn't until the 1950s that the leisure industry really started taking off again and the railway's seaside posters reflected that. Posters featured women in bathing suits, beachballs with smiley faces, children on donkeys. They offered a glimpse of a different kind of world.

My mother's family was just one of many seduced by the posters to take the train south. When they weren't hiding from the rain in the Redcar bandstand, my mum, her sister and their parents would stay in a caravan in Sandown, a seaside town on the east coast of the Isle of Wight. One year, my grandma sent money away every month as part of a deal in the *Daily Herald* for a fortnight in a caravan park on the Isle of Wight.

It was only when they got there they realised it had been a con. The company advertising it in the newspaper were not legit, and when my grandparents showed the relevant paperwork to the owners of the caravan park, they were baffled and had to tell them no such accommodation existed. In the end my grandparents had to knock on the door of every bed and breakfast in town in the hope there was somewhere they could stay. There was no luck until one nativity-scene-innkeeper type allowed them the use of the one free room in his house. The next morning my mum saw him coming out of the bathroom with a pillow and a blanket: he'd sacrificed his own bed for them, sleeping in the bath.

Not everyone was as accommodating about the nation's holiday plans. In the early 1960s, the railways found themselves the victims of some brutal government cuts. The Stockton to Redcar train, like so many others, fell victim to Dr Beeching, who chopped up the railways of Great Britain single handed and used them as firewood to light a fat cigar. Although he was acting on government instructions, it is his name that remains synonymous with the decline of something special that people loved. Due to the Beeching Axe, many stations were forced to close down and much-loved routes were blocked off. Train travel, and to some extent the seaside, was never the same again.

As we set out from the station for the seafront, my mum attempted to gather her bearings. So many of our seaside memories are from knee height rather than being fully grown.

'It's difficult with all these roadworks,' she said, looking all around her.

For miles and miles we could see nothing but scaffolding, traffic cones, red triangular signs. Beyond all of that, apparently, there was a beach. Locally the area had been struggling, experiencing what local Labour MP Mark Hannon described as 'a scourge of unemployment'. Like many seaside resorts, Redcar had stagnated over the previous two or three generations.

Unlike some other seaside resorts, though, Redcar was not being allowed to wither and die. The town was at the beginning of an exciting adventure: a 15-year development scheme was in its very early stages, which included £30 million sea defences, plans to build a community centre and a futuristic looking 'vertical pier'. This was an 80-foot structure which when built would house artists and creative businesses, with a public viewing platform at the top. We had already passed several posters for this; they were everywhere on the seafront, next to the signs apologising for the inconvenience of the building works. It was estimated that the regeneration of Redcar would attract an extra one million visitors annually.

'Let's try this way,' my mum suggested. We walked along the promenade, past the statue of a director's chair, erected to commemorate the filming of the adaptation of Ian McEwan's novel *Atonement* on Redcar Beach. This was no embellished story devised to trick tourists. The town had in fact played a huge role in the filming – it wasn't that the crew were shooting nearby and on her day off Keira Knightly or James McAvoy had been there for an afternoon and bought a can of Apple Tango and a *Daily Express* from the newsagents. On Redcar beach thousands of extras had dressed as soldiers depicting the Dunkirk evacuation scenes. During the filming, Redcar had experienced an increase of around 70 per cent in the number of tourists, who had visited the town's promenade to see the film being shot.

My mum and I negotiated the confusing layout the roadworks had created around Redcar seafront and were able to find Pacitto's. The café can hardly have changed in the last 40 years; it still sold its menu of Kit Kats and Wagon Wheels and Bovril. Also going strong was the Pacitto family claim to be the creators of 'the original Lemon Top: dairy ice cream in a cone, with a blob of lemon sorbet on top'.

I drank a vanilla float, which was a cup of coffee with a scoop of ice cream in it. My mum just had a cup of tea because she's sensible. On another table, two grandparents were treating their grandson to an enormous knickerbocker glory. He practically had to stand on his chair to be able to reach into it. Anything that involves a long spoon is always exciting. When we used to go to Pacitto's as children we always used to ask for ice cream sodas: lemonade with a scoop of ice cream in it. These Pacitto guys loved dolloping ice cream into places you wouldn't normally dollop ice cream.

As she drank her tea and a blob of ice cream unsatisfactorily melted in my cup of coffee, my mum talked about her holidays when she was young, fond memories of growing up in the North East, although a lot of the memories did seem to be dominated by rain.

'Redcar was where we'd go for a half day,' she explained. 'If we went away for a full day it would be Whitby. Your grandma used to buy what were called Train Runabout Tickets, which meant you could go anywhere in the area for a week. We'd have to go to Whitby every day just to get our money's worth.'

Day trips were particularly important in helping the feel-good factor between the two wars. There was a nationwide determination to carry on life as normal and the seaside was the ideal place to make that happen. In the post-war period the falling cost of living and the sense of this newly found freedom after so much time worrying and being housebound meant people were keen to explore. At the same time these explorations tended to be limited to the UK, and that wasn't just for financial and logistical reasons. It was seen as unpatriotic to go abroad. The majority of the children in the same class as my mum at school holidayed in Britain.

Redcar was also remembered fondly by the late Mo Mowlam. Mowlam was the MP for the town between 1987 and 2001 and rarely has a politician been so synonymous with their constituency, with the *Observer* dubbing her the 'Queen of Redcar'. In her autobiography, *Momentum*, Mowlam described her house on the seafront and how she was able to sit up in bed and watch the sea: 'However difficult or tough times were in Westminster,' she wrote, 'that always put life into perspective.'

It wasn't just the pressures of Westminster that people were escaping from in Redcar. Times had been tough growing up in the North East, with the decline of the traditional industries the area had prided itself on. Towns that had grown out of the Industrial Revolution were less prosperous in a world of blogs and smartphones. For Mo Mowlam, my mum and others like them, little could beat a day on Redcar Beach. As Mowlam put it: 'The sea is constant and strong and makes other things seem petty.'

What changed in the nation's holidaying patterns to take people away from the seaside? It's not as if the weather is any different to when my parents or grandparents were growing up: it rained then just as it does now. The difference is that in the past people had little choice other than just to tolerate it, soldiering on with their holidays regardless. Back then, for most people going abroad wasn't a realistic possibility.

The reasons for so many empty patches on British beaches, the lack of queues at the ice cream stands, is because people are at Gatwick, Heathrow and Humberside airports. Well, not so much Humberside, but definitely the others. It wasn't singularly Ryanair which changed British holiday patterns, but they are the most newsworthy example and a useful collective noun. Ryanair is a company which regularly attracts the attention of both broadsheets and tabloids, and so has become the figurehead, the shorthand for anything to do with cheap flights abroad. The group's philosophy can be summed up by its CEO Michael O'Leary's piece of wisdom about the need for baggage handlers: 'Get rid of all that crap,' he told Bloomburg.com in 2010. 'You take your own bag with you. You bring it down. You put it on.'

A lot of what budget airlines try to push on their customers is the antithesis of everything a holiday should involve. There used to be so much glamour in going away on your holidays. These days, it seems as though the enjoyment is being sucked out of it. In an interview with *Newsweek* magazine in 2010, O'Leary said, 'The physical process of getting from point A to point B shouldn't be pleasant, nor enriching. It should be quick, efficient, affordable, and safe.' But by being so ruthless surely we are missing out on something. Holidays should always feel a privilege, a treat. They are a reward for working hard all year, and the point of earning money is to relax when you get the chance. Don't look at the prices on the menu. Have an ice cream even if you don't want one. Drink too much. Buy a silly hat. Feel full and contented when you go to bed and fresh and enthusiastic when you get up in the morning. Relax. Enjoy yourself. It is about escapism. This was never truer than in the post-war years. In 1945, Winston Churchill urged the nation to take a break, get away for a few days and celebrate the end of the Second World War.

The image of a Prime Minister instructing people to take a break now feels like something from a bygone age. It was like a concerned parent worrying about their studious kid revising too much for their GCSEs. Winston Churchill was encouraging a nation to go and get some fresh air, have a bike ride, take a long walk. At the time there was typically a fortnight's holiday granted by employers every year. We are spoiled in the 21st century.

I spoke to my friends who were about to go on holiday abroad and some who had just returned. They all agreed there was a sense of peril involved with packing the suitcase at the end of the holiday, going home and putting a wash on. As soon as they set foot in the arrivals lounge back in the UK there was a feeling of doom. This is exactly what I was trying to avoid with my seaside journey. Two weeks in the Bahamas has its temptations, but I preferred a different type of holiday: weekends, day trips, a few days here and there on the British coast – all the advantages of having a break without ever needing to travel too far or be away from home for too long.

Redcar suffered as much as any resort when holidaying at the British seaside started to become less popular. Now, though, things were looking up. In 1999, Chris Smith, the then Minister for Culture, singled out Redcar as 'a town on a depressed coastline which had successfully reinvented itself'. As well as the seafront redevelopment scheme, a deal had been done to get the steel works running again, giving employment to many of the several hundred workers who had been laid off when the original contract ended.

Things had been grim for Redcar for a while, but now there was a huge sense of optimism, or at least there would be once those roadworks had been completed. Maybe with the right investment, British seaside resorts could once again be as big as they were in the 1960s. Maybe the days of the budget airlines and the novelty of cheap holidays abroad will not last forever.

My mum and I watched the little boy eating his knickerbocker glory from a glass which was not much smaller than him.

'Can we go in the sea later?' he asked.

'Maybe,' his grandparents replied, even though the answer was clearly a resounding no.

'Can we go on the donkeys? Can we go on Thomas?'

As we walked back to the train station the theme tune to *Thomas the Tank Engine* played across the arcade. Maybe life isn't changing as dramatically as we sometimes fear.

CHAPTER THREE

Mr and Mrs Cleethorpes Entertainment

My next trip to the seaside took to me to another North Sea resort with family connections. I had been at my mum and dad's for a few days after our trip to Redcar so I decided to go across to Cleethorpes, as I had done so many times before. It seemed a long time since I'd driven the 20 miles down the A180 and I was eager to know if my less fond memories held true.

Even from a young age I could tell Cleethorpes was a bit crap. It had been a popular holiday destination in the 1950s, but by the end of the 20th century it was run down and generally considered an embarrassment by many locals. It was so bad when I was growing up that we looked forward to seeing people's faces when we took them to visit. 'Let's show them Cleethorpes,' we'd say whenever we had to entertain cousins, German exchange students or friends from university.

Cleethorpes is just a short walk from Grimsby, which is where we used to go to buy our school uniforms, and as such I have never had much of a fondness for it there. There can't have been a single Christmas Eve in the 1990s that I hadn't spent in Woolworths in Grimsby, desperately in search of last-minute presents as that Paul McCartney Christmas song played on, regardless.

Growing up, it always seemed that Cleethorpes was somewhere nothing happened, apart from an occasional Radio 1 Roadshow. There wasn't much glamour to the place: notable people to have lived in Cleethorpes included Ian Huntley, Norman Lamont's mother and the actress who played Mrs Mangle in *Neighbours*. It was here, too, that I first saw blue light bulbs in a public toilet. I remember asking my dad on one visit why they had blue light bulbs. He explained it was so heroin addicts couldn't see their veins in order to inject more heroin. Then we went home.

Yet there had been a time when Cleethorpes had been a 'go-to' destination for earlier generations. Like Redcar, Cleethorpes had benefited from the railways and their marketing campaigns. One poster depicts one man leapfrogging another as families play with beachballs with the slogan 'Cleethorpes: It's Quicker By Rail.' One of those who used to visit (though on coach trips, rather than by train) was my grandma.

'Cleethorpes!' we'd laughed in her face. The place seemed no more a holiday destination than an Asda car park, or a central reservation. Surely she was mistaken. My grandma, though, explained that things were different in The Old Days. She told us about the lack of choice and the group coach trips; the sense of anticipation and the songs they would sing. Her face lit up as she taught us the songs. I think I'd have been perfectly happy a few decades earlier: the stories my grandma told me always sounded so cheerful, an idyllic way to spend your summer, an era before too many bright colours and shapes and airport departure lounges. Maybe, then, there was something about Cleethorpes that I had missed. That was what I was hoping to uncover on my trip.

The 'sea' at Cleethorpes is actually the mouth of the Humber. At low tide you can see nothing but mud; not a particularly refreshing prospect as you run towards it in your Speedos. Even in the most glorious sunshine the beach is dank: the sun in the grey sky has a speech bubble from its painted face saying 'I'm so sorry about this.'

I parked up by the beach. Although it was out of season, like all seaside towns Cleethorpes still had the mentality of Manhattan when it came to the importance of parking places: 'Is he coming out? No, he's just straightening up. Bastard.' Beaches can inspire some weird behaviour – 'We're not going home. Remember how long it took us to find our parking space.'

Walking down Central Promenade, an arcade played *Papa Don't Preach*. A little girl sat in a red post van next to

Postman Pat and Jess. On big claw machines you could win ugly, bastardised cuddly toy versions of Winnie-the-Pooh, Scooby-Doo and Mickey Mouse. It was hard to remember which decade we were in. A girl sat on a carousel horse. She was too old for this. Her face said she wanted to go home. Two Alsatians flirted outside the arcade.

'I want an ice cream,' another little girl said outside Johnny Donuts ice cream parlour. You're supposed to say please. You can only get a 99 if you behave. That's the rule. It was in Cleethorpes I first learnt that it's only a 99 if it's a Cadbury's Flake. The name 99 refers to the flake rather than the ice cream. There is a certain type of person who will always point that out to you, in the same way they will say Big Ben is the name of the bell, not of the clock. It's not a Tannoy, it's a public address system.

Cleethorpes has not always been a pleasant town to walk around. In 2011, the *Grimsby Telegraph* reported on a planning row over whether the shutters of an empty shop on Cleethorpes' high street made it look like a 'war zone'. The owners of the shop were being forced to remove the security shutters after members of North East Lincolnshire Council's planning committee ruled they were not in keeping with the area's conservation plan. Councillor David Hornby, who voted for the removal of the shutters, said, 'We are talking about Cleethorpes here; a tourist destination ... those shutters are appalling and they should be changed.'

So much of the area was in decline I worried it was in freefall, but the council's stand was proof that there was some attention being paid, on some level it was being cared for. Further down the promenade, too, I found an unexpected tranquillity – the first real clue that Cleethorpes might not be all bad. This was the Lakeside development, an area you could quite easily miss. It was across the way from a KFC and a McDonald's, whose unavoidable mess and debris was blowing across the dual carriageway in the breeze towards the lake, something unappetising for the ducks to peck at.

I watched as a little girl with her dad threw pieces of Hovis into the lake. Nothing is more fun for a toddler than ripping off pieces of bread, throwing them for ducks to enjoy. As I walked past the little girl – the crumbs from her loaf providing a big attraction to anything feathered within a five-mile radius – I realised I was convinced the ducks were going to kill me. A new phobia to deal with. How annoying.

There was a special bird-feeding area. The information board advised that if you are going to feed the birds with bread you should make sure it's wholemeal. Even the ducks are conscious of their waistlines these days. I'm sure I saw one of them in the promenade café earlier, reading *Grazia* and insisting their latte was served with soya.

On the wall of the boating lake office there were plaques next to the model boat sailing times. Generally, death is tucked away, towards the back of newspapers, avoided in conversation. At seasides, though, the subject tends to be at the forefront, impossible to avoid, like these dedications to those who spent their days relaxing by the Cleethorpes lake: *In memory of Desmond Fox, retired naval man and model boat builder. Still looking over the boats. In memory of Roy Hartell. Clockmaker and model builder. A time for sailing.*

By the water a man in a flat cap controlled a model boat. That'll be me when I'm older: sitting on a bench using my remote to navigate it left and right, thinking about maybe getting some chips. I'd be happy with that one day. I'd be quite happy with that now.

Walking back to the seafront you pass a fenced-off area, a seaside mural, painted either by local schoolchildren or a cutting-edge young artist. It can be hard to tell sometimes. This is what used to be one of the resort's most recognisable and famous landmarks: Cleethorpes Winter Gardens.

There must be a generation of couples who are together as a result of evenings spent at Winter Garden dances at seaside resorts across the UK; long walks by the seafront, walking home hand in hand afterwards. Winter Gardens are generally grandiose, expensive, vast buildings with dance halls and floral gardens. In their day they hosted tea dances, brass bands and social gatherings. They were mostly built around the turn of the century, a time when seaside resorts were being developed and weren't shy with the extravagance of the buildings.

It was not uncommon to have a Winter Gardens back in the day. Weston-super-Mare's Gardens are described as 'the focal point of the community who for many years dined, danced and socialised there'. Eastbourne Winter Gardens is a Grade II listed building built in 1875. The Blackpool Winter Gardens Company was registered in the same year, its intentions to build 'a pleasant lounge, especially desirous during inclement days'. Margate Winter Gardens, meanwhile, made the most of its concert and dance hall. In the early 1920s, the Margate Municipal Orchestra, consisting of 36 musicians, would perform. After the war, performers included high-profile names such as Vera Lynn and Laurel and Hardy.

The story of the history of Cleethorpes Winter Gardens is as romantic as any of its rivals. Back in 1934, a lady called Rose Eyre owned a plot of land. Her husband George had an accident while working on the railway, resulting in both his legs needing to be amputated. He received substantial compensation as a result of his injuries, and the couple decided they would use it to finance a new building that was to be called Olympia: permission was granted for an 'amusement hall and restaurant'. After his injuries George Eyre was able to get around Cleethorpes in his wheelchair, which was pushed by his friend Owen Stanland. Stanland loved roller skating, so when they were designing the building George and Rose Eyre decided to order flooring suitable for roller skating, as a thank-you to their friend. It was at one of the early roller dances that Owen Stanland met his future wife. A roller-skating romance.

After the Second World War the building reopened and was renamed the Winter Gardens. Its manager was Don Twidale, who was also a baker. He'd get up at dawn every morning to start baking, get his horse and cart and deliver bread and cakes to his customers in Cleethorpes and beyond. Twidale created his own musical ensemble from local talent, who performed as the Winter Gardens Orchestra on Sunday nights.

Another tale of romance from the Winter Gardens is that of Jack Lawton, an organist during summer seasons on Cleethorpes Pier. One day a girl called Shirley King arrived for a singing audition. She soon earned the nickname 'the East Coast's answer to Vera Lynn'. Jack and Shirley fell in love and the couple married in 1963. They became a double act and started performing together at a 'nostalgia night' variety show at the Winter Gardens. The couple became well known locally as 'Mr and Mrs Cleethorpes Entertainment'. On Friday afternoons they hosted tea dances. Shirley King eventually took over the post of marketing and promotions manager for the Winter Gardens until her retirement in 1996.

To find out more about Cleethorpes Winter Gardens I had contacted a man who has been associated with them for much of his life. Steve Jackson is a music journalist for the *Grimsby Telegraph* and someone with a first-hand knowledge of the venue's history.

'It was just a Mecca for live music,' he told me over the phone, his Lincolnshire accent reassuring and familiar. 'Bus companies would put on special buses because the gigs weren't over 'til late. At the end of the night I'd go back home, a 40-minute walk by the sea. I was 16 when I went to that first gig at the Winter Gardens and I've been obsessed with live music ever since.'

Steve was born in Cleethorpes but grew up in Canada when his parents emigrated there when he was small. They moved back to the UK when he was 15. It was the late 1960s and as a young teenager who had seen London and Liverpool on the television, he thought returning to Britain would be the coolest place to be. But this wasn't London or Liverpool. It was Cleethorpes.

'I remember seeing rows and rows of grim terraced housing,' Steve recalled. 'I was living at my granny's house with an outside loo. But Cleethorpes Winter Gardens saved me.'

This was where Steve watched live music for the first time. As with many local people his record collection was built from those bands that appeared at the Winter Gardens. They saw people they'd only previously read about in the *New Musical Express* and *Melody Maker*. Steve got himself a haircut and a pair of drainpipes and went to every gig he could.

'I can remember everything so vividly,' he told me. 'The equipment, the way people dressed, the smells. There was always a smell of food, permeated in the woodwork. It was *oveny*. I can smell it now, just as I can see the ladies serving behind the bar, refusing to smile, their eyes scalding the boys with long hair.'

'John Peel DJ'd at the Winter Gardens,' Steve continued. 'He brought his record collection along, with his long hair, wearing his Creedence Clearwater Revival shirt. You could go over to him and say hello and then he'd be back on his Radio 1 show talking about it the following night. Sometimes there were bands like Atomic Rooster and

Uriah Heep, who'd do things like have exploding dustbins on stage with them for effects. The Winter Gardens must be responsible for lots of people in North Lincolnshire in their fifties now with hearing problems.' Another famous band to have played there was Queen, in 1974. They were supposed to have played the Winter Gardens earlier, but allegedly that gig was cancelled by the band as there was no grand piano available.

It seems all the punk bands went to Cleethorpes in the late 1970s. Generation X. The Damned. The Stranglers had to spend the night in Grimsby jail after a fracas. Steve said he occasionally felt in genuine danger: 'I once saw a cymbal thrown from the stage, flying through the crowd. If it had hit someone it would have decapitated them! The punk gigs were shambolic; thrashing the hell out of three chords.'

But those gigs weren't about the music. They were about the occasion. Most famously of all The Sex Pistols came to the Winter Gardens as part of their 1976 *Anarchy in the UK* tour. Steve remembers a threat about it all, an unsettling menace. There were demonstrations outside: lots of venues had cancelled their appearance because their reputation was becoming increasingly negative. The venue managers were scared and stopped the gigs from happening. Not in Cleethorpes, though. The previous night there had been a dinner dance with the Mayor in attendance, ballroom dancing during the afternoon. The next night it was The Sex Pistols and The Clash on the same bill. The place had a few blokes from the docks; Grimsby folk looking for trouble. But mostly it was people there for a good night, some beers, your ears ringing as you stopped for chips on the way home.

For Steve and hundreds like him, the Winter Gardens were a lifeline. These people were coming to their town, a bit of glamour and excitement in Cleethorpes. Then they'd load their van up, drive away and it was back to work until the next band came along.

It wasn't just the punk movement that the Winter Gardens were quick to be involved with. Steve went to watch Rik Mayall at the Winter Gardens and it was sold out. Seven hundred people watching a guy talking into a microphone: comedy was becoming the new rock and roll and again Cleethorpes was at the heart of it. Northern Soul club nights in Cleethorpes, too, were a success and seriously rivalled the famous nights at Wigan Casino. Then there was Screaming Lord Sutch, who played there too shortly before he died: the teddy boys of Lincolnshire were out in force supporting one of the greatest eccentrics in British history.

Other great gigs stick in Steve's mind. 'The night Dexys Midnight Runners played was the week *Geno* was the number one single,' he told me. 'It tended to be Thursdays that bands were put on, so everyone watched Dexys on *Top of the Pops*, then went down to the Winter Gardens to see them perform live. That's pretty special. That's the kind of thing you don't get nowadays.'

For all the musical history the Winter Gardens had to offer, there was to be no encore. On 12 February 2007, the long-running fight to halt its demolition was lost. The Winter

Gardens was boarded up and scheduled for demolition, and the inevitable happened over that summer, the wrecking ball smashing roller-skating and Sex Pistols memories to smithereens. There had been numerous calls and petitions to save the Winter Gardens. These were ignored, though, as most petitions are. North East Lincolnshire Council refused to consider a replacement venue or remove the planning permission to demolish. Instead of the Winter Gardens the development of new apartments was started … and then stopped. This was halted by the economic downturn and the site of the Winter Gardens was used as a temporary car park: £3 a day. Memories are inconsequential when it comes to (admittedly cheap) parking.

The story of Cleethorpes Winter Gardens is, unfortunately, far from unique. Although Winter Gardens still exist across the country, most that do are struggling and many, like Cleethorpes, have been demolished completely. One of the biggest buildings ever to grace an English seafront, the Southport Winter Gardens, was not a great commercial success. It was converted into a ballroom and roller-skating rink, before being demolished. The site was used for a model village before it made way for a shopping development. The site is now occupied by a Morrisons car park.

'I still get nostalgic when I go past where the Winter Gardens used to be,' Steve told me. 'It's just a flattened space, but back then you could meet your music heroes; all these people on their way to the top. I really feel that Cleethorpes played its part in musical history. It was a different era. The venue was just as important before punk, during the 1950s and 60s. But as time went on it became less and less special, stopped attracting the big names and it was all tribute bands and people who have been on *The X Factor*. It's not right.'

Steve agreed that there was no way we would ever see anything like the Winter Gardens again. But just because the Winter Gardens don't exist any more and the ubiquity of bland pop music is everywhere doesn't mean there is no room for creative and interesting work. Steve, it transpired, performed across Lincolnshire as Strummin' Steve Jackson – 'folky, jiggy stuff'. He organised music events whenever he could and says it's all because of those early days at the Winter Gardens. During Live Aid he put together a Cleethorpes Winter Gardens night to coincide with Geldof and his mates.

'Why would you build a Winter Gardens now?' Steve asked. 'You'd struggle with your business plan. The world has changed and you can't re-create what we once had. You embrace new things. That's the wonder of life. Technology evolves and you run with it. All these bands I used to go and watch, they have been preserved because of sites like YouTube. Who'd have thought that all that footage would be available to watch in your own home? My kids can watch the bands I used to watch. I think that's a pretty spectacular thing. So although it is devastating there isn't a Winter Gardens any more, look at the things we do have. The one thing that does make me sad is that there isn't something to commemorate the site. I'd like to see a blue plaque there. That would be fitting.'

As it turns out, Cleethorpes deserves not one blue plaque for its place in musical history, but two.

'Did you know the guy who wrote *Thriller* is from Cleethorpes?' my friend Dan had asked, when I told him where I was going.

That blew my mind. It's true. *Thriller,* the Michael Jackson track credited as the song that revolutionised music, was written by a man called Rod Temperton from Cleethorpes. Rod left school and got a job working in a frozen fish factory in Grimsby. In 1974, he answered an advert in the back of *Melody Maker,* resulting in him joining the band Heatwave. The band did well, with Rod writing all the songs. He was spotted by legendary producer Quincy Jones, who asked him to work with Michael Jackson. He wrote lots of lyrics, but Jones wasn't happy with the title of one song, *Starlight.* So Rod sat down in his hotel room and came up with hundreds of alternative titles and, as he recalls, 'One morning I woke up and I just said this word. Something in my head just said, "This is the title." You could visualise it at the top of the Billboard charts. You could see the merchandising for this one word, how it jumped off the page as *Thriller.*'

Thriller is the title track of the best-selling studio album in the United States and has sold well over 100 million copies worldwide. And it was all written by a guy from Cleethorpes. To be fair, he also wrote the song *I'm That Chick* by Mariah Carey, so maybe we shouldn't give him too much praise.

The more people I told this *Thriller* fact, the more I found out about other seaside claims to fame. Busta Rhymes, the man behind the track *Woo-Hah!! Got You All In Check,* grew up in Brooklyn, New York, but was regularly sent to his aunt's house in Morecambe to stop him from getting in trouble. Local legend says he stole a pair of trainers from a shop during his stay there and was sent back by his aunt to apologise. The shop made him clean the floors as a punishment. As far as I know Public Enemy have never been to Whitstable. NWA haven't spent any time in Whitby. I also imagine Rod Temperton doesn't live in Cleethorpes any more.

As I walked around Cleethorpes, with all the people bustling past us doing their last bits of shopping before the stores shut, I thought about 'Mr and Mrs Cleethorpes Entertainment', about Steve and his many musical memories of Cleethorpes. Sometimes, I realised, we take the seaside for granted. We fail to appreciate the places we grew up. The town near my house that I once regarded as simply a place where nothing happens, I will now never be able to think of without the bassline from *Thriller* running through my body.

CHAPTER FOUR

Skegness Is So Bracing

Skegness – Skeggie, as it's called by locals – is not too far from Cleethorpes, less than an hour by car. Both towns suffer from the same problem as other towns in the Humberside area; that they sound pretty unappealing. One story that made the news was when David Harper, a leading property consultant, said that the name Skegness came with too much baggage, and should be changed. As was reported on the BBC website, he said, 'Most of the people I speak to, who don't know Skegness, think it's one of the grottier resorts in the country.' He suggested it needed to be re-branded to attract a wealthier market: changing its name would be a cost effective way of reinventing the town. '[People] have a perception of it being all caravans and slot machines. They have no clue that it has one of the best beaches there in the whole of the UK.'

Despite only being an hour down the road, I had never visited either Skegness or its own particular piece of seaside history: the original Butlins resort. This was to be my first visit to a holiday camp, but my mum told me that she used to go quite regularly, not on holiday but in her capacity as a French teacher. For a few years, as part of the glamorously titled Lincolnshire County Council's Technical and Vocational Education Initiative, hundreds of local schoolchildren would arrive on buses at a completely revamped Butlins for French Days, designed to help GCSE pupils with their French exams. It was a chance to improve language skills.

Teachers like my mum would have to work at the stalls, selling food or working in the shop or at the makeshift bureau de change, where the no doubt reluctant Lincolnshire schoolchildren had to exchange English money for francs. French music would play from the speakers, all the signs would have been specially remade in French, and there would be fines given out by teachers who heard any pupil not speaking French. At the end of the day there would be a talent show where all participants had to perform in French.

This was during the 1980s when holiday camps were really suffering. In 1978, Butlins' main rival, Pontins, had been sold by their founder Fred Pontin to the betting company Coral, then a couple of years later to the brewing company Bass. It was a time when holiday camps across the UK, as well as bed and breakfasts, hotels and seaside businesses, were closing down, changing hands, and no-one was quite sure what to do.

Unlike many other businesses, however, Butlins was able to come out on the other side, survive the '80s and recover from the downturn. I was keen to discover how they had managed this, and to find out for myself what it was like inside a modern holiday camp.

It was on a drizzly Wednesday in October that I made my visit. First of all I stopped off in Skegness itself, which is as glitzy and kitsch as any seaside resort in the UK. A huge sign across the pier has the words *Skegness Pier: What a great idea!* A nearby café has a sign on its outdoor wall: *Due to a limited number of tables, if you are not a customer of Whippie Dippes or The Snack Station you will be asked to leave NO EXCEPTIONS. Thank you.* It was not the slot machines or the hospitality I was in Skegness for, though, it was Butlin's. Traditionally this would have been a time when holiday camps closed down for the winter. Due to the lack of heating they were only open 16 weeks a year. Now Butlin's is open 50 weeks a year, which means across the three remaining Butlin's there are still as many visitors as there were back in their peak in their heyday of the 1950s and 60s, when there were nine Butlin's spread across the UK.

Families taking advantage of the half-term holiday weren't the only ones making a visit in October: the previous weekend they had five and a half thousand people on site for a Seventies weekend. The following week there would be the same amount of people for brass band entertainment.

I had a wander around, to take in the Butlin's experience. Maintenance and building work were being carried out, people marched with a purpose, wearing tool belts or climbing up ladders or drilling. The chalets families stayed in looked cosy. There was a pub with Sky Sports on big screens to watch the football. That must have a special atmosphere during the World Cup. There was a newsagents: 'Let's get some scratch cards. We're on holiday!' A postbox, postcards sent away in their millions: 'Having a lovely time in Skegness.' There was a spa – health and relaxation. A Costa Coffee, obviously. Papa John's Pizza, a go-kart racing track, hook-a-duck, carousels with loyal golden horses, stoically going round and round for generations. Billy's Ices, the ice cream van, was a nod to the resort's founder, Billy Butlin. The rides looked fun. Enough to keep you out of trouble for an hour or two. Most famous of all were the dodgems. Butlin was the man who introduced dodgems to the UK.

After the mini-funfair I went indoors to the Pavilion. I'm sure there's been many a gin and tonic drunk in the Yacht Club, the higher end bar where parents reward themselves for putting up with screaming kids all day. 'At 8pm I can have a Bombay Sapphire,' they say, looking at their watch as the kids are playing on the dance mat. In the mini-supermarket the booze fridge was well stocked. A man sat behind a table selling wood carvings. Next to him, a lady had a stall displaying brooches. These people were here for the grandparents, every bit on holiday as the little kids running around. Maybe they remembered the days when they were running around underneath the same roof all those years ago.

On the main stage, *Imagine with Benny* was going on. This consisted of a big bear in a red dress, being led around stage by two girls who were about 18, and who couldn't stop giggling. A little girl near me burst into tears, hugging her mum, on hand to save her from the terrifying bear. All the other children seemed to love it: at the front of the audience was a group of toddlers dancing around, having the time of their life. They adored Benny. There must have been so many different performers on that stage throughout the years. People on stage, making audiences laugh. Entertaining strangers who had worked hard all year and had come to Skegness on their holiday, their special summer treat.

Benny waved goodbye, they played his exit music and everyone went to Burger King for their lunch.

Chris Baron, the resort manager, had kindly agreed to see me and tell me a little about the resort's history. His office was the engine room of the Skegness site, and he invited me in to tell me the remarkable story of the camp's founder: Billy Butlin.

'He was the equivalent to Richard Branson,' Chris explained, but even that doesn't quite seem to do justice to the man whose name is still so synonymous with British holidays. So much of the success Butlin achieved in life was driven by his personality. He designed the Skegness camp himself, largely based on sketches and ideas he doodled on the backs of cigarette packets.

Butlin was born in 1899. His family were both wealthy and eccentric: his father was described as 'a well-educated man and a typical country gentleman of his time, who never expected to work and spent most of his time playing tennis'. Butlin's mother was the daughter of a banker who had become a travelling showman. The marriage ended (which is likely to happen if you devote your entire life to playing tennis), and Billy and his mum travelled around summer fairs in her caravan running a gingerbread stall for her brother Marshall. His mum remarried and emigrated with her husband to Canada, where Billy later joined them. He never wanted to have a normal life, it was something he always rebelled from. After the First World War he ended up setting up a darts stall at the Toronto Exhibition.

When Billy moved back to England he started to work on the fairgrounds. Soon he was doing so well he could afford to fly his mum in from Canada. It was then he moved to the seaside: 'One day Billy Butlin was in a pub in London and saw two men, well-dressed and wealthy,' Chris explained. 'He was intrigued, found out they were from Skegness, so he thought he'd come and have a look, and that changed this town forever.'

To begin with, Butlin leased a piece of land at Skegness to run funfairs on the seafront; when the problem arose that it was full of sand dunes, he simply advertised the sand for sale, and buyers had to collect it themselves, not realising they were effectively doing manual labour for him for free. This was the perfect example of turning a problem into an opportunity. (I have the same ability but in reverse.) Then he bought a 200-acre field, and in 1936 the first Butlin's opened in Skegness. Butlin became famous across the UK: what was once a turnip field became the prototype for a way to change holidays forever.

When I was there the car park was full, but when the Skegness resort opened in 1936 people would arrive on the train by the carriage-load. They'd throw their stuff onto a big lorry, get the bus down, meet the lorry at the resort and get their stuff back. There would also be barrow boys at the station with their barrows, meeting people and taking them to the seaside or their accommodation.

The secret of Billy Butlin's success was his observation of British life. His amusement parks caught on because he knew what people wanted when they went on holiday. The idea developed from his observation of the seaside landladies who used to throw their guests out between mealtimes, no matter how bad the weather was. He remembered seeing the hordes of holidaymakers wandering around in the rain with nowhere to go. There wasn't really an alternative holiday destination, so he made one himself.

The glory days of the 1950s and 60s weren't to last. Butlin's was forced to make closures as the 20th century drew to an end, unable to compete with the lure of cheap flights abroad. Going to a holiday camp just wasn't something people did any more. They had become so shrouded with preconceptions that it was hard to ascertain what they were actually like. But being there gave me the chance to see it for myself and I was impressed. Despite the reduction nationwide from nine sites to three, the Butlin's tradition seems well placed to continue. This is a different world to the one seen in *Hi-de-Hi!*, the British sitcom about holiday camps co-written by Jimmy Perry, himself once a Redcoat at Butlin's. There have been significant changes since the days depicted by Ruth Madoc and Su Pollard – to the extent that Butlin's no longer use the words 'holiday camp' when they describe themselves. One of the three remaining Butlin's is in Bognor Regis, where there was a big undertaking to keep the resort a viable option for holidaygoers. This has meant getting rid of the famous Butlin's chalets. In 2009 the Ocean Hotel opened, which, intriguingly features a 'disco lift, allowing guests to travel between floors in style'. Most excitingly of all, the hotel has 'disco showers'. It turns out disco showers might be the key to counter the economic downturn.

I wondered whether the recession would have been a boost for Butlin's but Chris wasn't so keen to give the credit to external forces. He said it was more because of Butlin's policy to invest heavily every year, particularly in marketing.

'We have to keep investing,' Chris told me. 'Our philosophy has always been to get returning guests. What they want to see is that for their holiday, 80 per cent is spent on this year's, 20 per cent on next. If it's as good as last year it'll be perceived as being worse. You always have to give them something that they'll go away thinking it was better. Billy was all about providing value for money, so I don't think we've moved that far away from his initial ideology of what Billy was doing, but as customers progress, we have to progress.'

The crucial mistake that resorts often make, Chris told me, is to mix adult groups with families. If a family is mixed in with a stag or hen party they'll never come back. If you're struggling, it's tempting to encourage as many people as possible to come to your resort because they spend well in bars. That, though, doesn't create an atmosphere for families. So you start to get a bad reputation at the weekends, and if a family doesn't come for the weekend they probably won't come midweek, for half-term or during the summer either.

'You have to take a long-term view,' Chris said. 'Skegness has always stuck to its family values. Butlin's is a traditional seaside resort. Family values were there at the start, we've maintained those and it seems to be working very well.'

Butlin's had also been very successful in recognising that a modern seaside resort is not all about the sea; from October to March they can look a bit more inwards, use their facilities to offer people a proper festival atmosphere without having to sleep in a tent. They have the apartments, catering and venues, and in the last few years they have become very smart about how to use their resources.

The Minehead Butlin's, for example, now hosts All Tomorrow's Parties in the winter. This is a music festival which started with a weekend curated by the band Belle and Sebastian back in 1999. The festival has featured bands such as Mogwai, Yeah Yeah Yeahs and Modest Mouse. The cool bands. All Tomorrow's Parties, named after a Velvet Underground song, describes itself as 'setting itself apart from other festivals by embracing seemingly disparate artistic genres'. I know it as the festival all the slightly cooler people than me go to. People who look cool in knitwear, who think Glastonbury isn't as good as it used to be, and who still buy their albums on vinyl.

There has been a boom in festivals in the 21st century and seaside resorts have often been a setting for them. For teenagers, music festivals provide the same function that holiday camps did in previous decades. Again it's about escapism. I've been to festivals every summer since I was 16 and loved it.

Spending time in a field in the middle of nowhere was what my friends and I always did; it's when we were at our happiest. This was our Mecca. Our Ibiza. Our Skegness.

Walking around the resort, it was clear there was little remaining from what people must perceive as being the glory days of Butlin's. What did remain was atmosphere. Some people seem to want the Butlin's they remember from their childhoods bottled; preserved forever. Whether that's from the *Hi-de-Hi!* days or when they went to resorts in the 1980s, they feel that nothing must change. It's just an unrealistic expectation.

Walking back outside again I saw a Redcoat! A real-life Redcoat! He was about 18, with lots of gel in his hair. He looked as if the best day of his life was when he found out that at school they were putting on a production of *Grease*, and that the worst was when he was cast as Eugene.

Redcoats were introduced by Butlin during the first ever week that his holiday camp was open, when he noticed that holidaymakers were genuinely struggling to enjoy themselves. They weren't used to having free time and suffered from an inability to relax: they might even have felt guilty about being allowed to do so. Originally, the Redcoats were just members of staff who were told to go and entertain those first holidaymakers, to do whatever occurred to them spontaneously to make sure that every single person who had paid money to be part of the Butlin's experience was having a good time. The Redcoats eventually became an institution, and people to have put on the red jacket and entertained include Des O'Connor, Michael Barrymore, Jimmy Tarbuck and William G Stewart from *Fifteen to One*. That was in the days when the holiday camp was thriving. In later years, H from Steps and Darren Day have been Redcoats. It would be cruel to say that those two individuals threatened to ruin holiday camps forever, but let's not rule that out as a possibility.

The Redcoat I saw was walking with his mate, a bear in a blue suit of armour, the two of them being pursued by a group of kids who wanted to have their photograph taken with him. The kids were screaming at the big blue bear, but for me the most exciting part of the whole day was seeing the Redcoat. He was having the best time. 'Guess what?' he'd have told his parents and friends on being offered the role. 'I'm going to be a Redcoat!'

On the wall in Chris's office had been a replica of the famous *Skegness Is So Bracing* poster, originally produced in 1908 by the Great Northern Railway. 'Skegness must be the most iconic poster,' Chris explained. 'Maybe I'm biased. There is no 21st-century marketing person who will come up with a similar slogan to Skegness Is So Bracing. It has a really nice feel to it.'

What the poster does suggest is something that is still true today – that Skegness is punching well above its weight as a seaside resort. It is never a holiday destination that is going to be universally liked, but so many television programmes and adverts and articles about seaside resorts mention Skegness, which is impressive for a small town with no infrastructure; most seaside resorts have a dual carriageway coming in and going out. Skegness doesn't have that.

'We're nowhere near the size of Brighton or Scarborough, but we're famous,' Chris had told me, proudly. 'Most people don't know where we are. Most think we're in Scotland, but we're really proud of what we've done. We are a small town but it's always in the top five seaside resorts in Great Britain because of the volume of people we attract. But if we ever sit on our laurels then we'll go backwards.'

That's true as much of the town as it is of the resort: 'If you took Butlin's away,' Chris continued, 'Skegness would really struggle. Clacton has really struggled since its Butlin's closed down. Other places have too. Skegness is lucky to have Butlin's. And Butlin's is lucky to have Skegness. If you go into Skegness and look around the seafront it is likely people will be wearing a Butlin's wristband. Very few shops in Skegness are closed down. That's because people at home do their retailing on the internet. When you're on holiday it's one of the very few times people are allowed to shop around. People like to walk around with bags, to fill their day shopping. Hopefully national chains will see this and invest more in seaside towns. When you're on holiday you've got the time.'

When I was growing up, we never went to holiday camps: Butlin's, Pontins or Haven. They always seemed bloody awful. But the Butlin's of today is something I would have been more interested in. There was none of the forced enjoyment that seemed prevalent in the 1980s. Walking around the site, I really understood what the modern-day Butlin's was doing. I bet those chalets were comfortable inside; as soon as you unlocked the door you could relax. You were on holiday. You might wander to the arcades or the dodgems, or to get some food or to the cinema. Everything was under one roof. You didn't need the sunshine. But if you did, the beach at Skegness was only three miles away; there was a taxi rank on site and shuttle buses regularly went to the seafront.

Butlin's seemed to be doing pretty well. A fun place to spend a holiday. A place where children, adults, grandparents were all genuinely relaxed, felt as if they had escaped their everyday lives. Most excitingly of all, there were Nice 'n' Spicy Nik Naks in the vending machine.

Part Two

EAST

CHAPTER FIVE

Can You Keep a Secret?

When people think of the seaside it's often the same few usual suspects. In a 2010 *Which?* magazine survey to find the best seaside towns, the top five were Blackpool, Brighton, Bournemouth, Whitby and Scarborough. That's a bit like saying 'If you like domestic pets, why not try cats and dogs?'

Articles are always appearing on websites or in glossy Sunday supplements containing lists of the best secret seaside towns, which is slightly paradoxical because as soon as the list is printed it is no longer a secret. What I was most looking forward to in my travels around the British coast was discovering the seaside resorts I had never heard of before, that existed for me only in books: places such as the lagoons at Holkham; Braunton Burrows, the UK's largest dune system, where Robbie Williams shot the video for *Angels*; Havergate Island, which you can only reach by the RSPB boat on the first Saturday of every month.

A few weeks previously I had been teaching in Aberdeen when I stumbled upon something that came as a genuine surprise seaside. 'Bloody hell, a beach!' I said to myself, much as if I'd just seen a stranger sitting on my settee. I didn't know there was a beach in Aberdeen, but suddenly I found myself on Beach Boulevard. Who knew there was a Beach Boulevard in Aberdeen? Admittedly there was a Matalan on Beach Boulevard, but I'm pretty sure that in Miami and Barbados there are Matalans leading up to the sandy beaches too.

I'd started my tour of the British coast by visiting the varied resorts of the North East. It had been a logical place to begin, given how places such as Scarborough, Redcar and Cleethorpes all came with family associations or fond childhood memories. But I was now living in East Anglia, so it was time to move on and discover my next area of the British coastline, widely acknowledged as one the most unspoilt pieces of land in the UK.

I was excited at the prospect. My travels in the North East had left me feeling much more knowledgeable about Britain, and now I had the chance to get to know better the area I had been living in for so long. Just as I'd not been to Skegness until recently, and knew so little about Cleethorpes, so the secret beaches of Norfolk had remained a mystery to me. It made sense to begin my journey down the East Anglian coastline by putting this right.

Hidden just a short drive from where I live are places such as Holkham and Wells-next-the-Sea, which are accessible only by car. When I told my friend Yanny that I was thinking about visiting these places, he said that he'd love to join me to go back there. Yanny had been to Holkham and Wells with his wife, his daughter, his friends when he was a student. When I was at university I rarely ventured further than the five-a-side Astroturf pitches. I had missed out on so much. There was nothing I could think of more enjoyable than driving around seasides with Yanny, so we jumped in the car and off we went. Yanny, as always, was the most delightful company imaginable: he was slightly older than me, much, much wiser, and the most gifted storyteller I have ever met. He put a tape he'd made for the journey in his tape player (he still uses tapes), I gave him a can of energy drink and told him to tell me about the old days.

First for me, Yanny and our two cans of Relentless was Holkham. I'd heard about its reputation as the best place to swim and to see seals, and that it was the perfect seaside. We parked up and went to the pay and display machine. In Britain we are lucky that our beaches are public – that isn't always the case in other countries. Many beaches in Italy are private: you have to know the right people to get a chance to sunbathe in certain areas, or pay extortionate amounts to do something we take for granted in Britain, albeit with much better weather. In some ways, though, Holkham is a private beach. It is impossible to get there without travelling by car, and the car park charge is £5.50, which acts as a way of saying, 'You are paying to get on this beach.' A man in a security booth was reading *Das Boot*, eating his sandwiches, looking like a film director's exposition of what a security guard looks like.

We walked down the track. I was grateful to have my own personal experienced guide to show me where to go. Looking around at the pine trees and as we continued along the vastness of the beach, it felt as if we were in Scandinavia rather than in Norfolk.

'So this is Holkham,' Yanny said after a good deal of walking, when we decided it was time to sit down and eat the sandwiches we'd brought with us. There are no facilities at Holkham. No toilets. No burger stand or arcade or somewhere to get a coffee. It felt as if it had been completely undiscovered. But that's only really a problem the first time you visit. There is no such thing as not having enough facilities. Only not having enough of a picnic.

We finished our sandwiches and carried on pootling along the beach. Once again, time was no object. While checking the clock is so crucial in towns and cities, in offices and cars, I had really found that in going to so many seaside resorts I was enjoying not being conscious of the time at all, to only have a rough stab at whether it was morning, afternoon or evening. Something special happens at the seaside. Something clicks inside your brain and relaxes you. It's a vital part of living and I don't think that's just for me. I've never been as relaxed about time, about whether or not I should be getting on with something else, than I was walking along Holkham Beach.

It was so cold as the two of us walked along: the thought of getting in the sea was as realistic as a spaceship landing beside us on the beach. There was no shelter anywhere, just the elements. Despite this it was still a busy place for people to spend their afternoon. Dog walkers, mainly. No-one walking their dogs seemed too stressed about life. One of the big attractions of Holkham is people riding freely on horseback. There were as many people riding horses as there were walking, and it seemed hard to believe that anywhere else could offer such freedom.

I really felt as if I'd missed out on never having been to Holkham despite living so close to it for ten years. Everything about the beach felt like a secret shared by me, Yanny and all the other people wandering around. As if we'd arrived via a portal. As if when we left we'd be asking the question of whether we'd ever been there at all. 'Did that just happen?'

The recurring theme of the seaside is that of escapism, and for some this involves wearing no clothes. Naturism has its origins in early 20th-century Germany and the trend quickly spread across the world, eventually, as all things do at some stage, reaching Norfolk. Holkham's naturist beach is among the most notable in the UK: 'One of my favourite places anywhere,' posted someone called Boris on a nudist beach forum.

Among the many debated topics regarding nudist bathing is whether or not to signpost the area. Although obviously it would help with being able to get there, the downside is that it attracts binocular-clad males who hover around. It's sad, and not helped in an age of *Babestation*, that some people are unable to separate nudism and sex. It's such a problem that the issue has even developed its own slang: these people who watch the nudist bathers are known as 'meerkats'; those who wear clothes in the nudist section are 'textiles'.

At Holkham there are just two signs for the nudist area, both of them small. In other places, the signage is more obvious. Morfa Dyffryn in Wales was used by naturists since the 1930s but it wasn't until 2000 that the local authority took the decision to put up notices designating the naturist section of the beach. This was deemed to be a success; the *Liverpool Daily Post* reported that the number of complaints about the naturists on this beach dropped 'from twenty in 1999 to only one in 2000 when the notices were visible and the naturists had their own part of the beach'.

For Yanny and me it was cold enough that day, even with our coats on. I imagined all the nudists were indoors, with a pot of tea and the fire on. One complaint about the naturist section of the beach at Holkham is that it is underused: it stretches on for so long, people are just scattered around and there is no sense of community.

The main attraction of Holkham, whether you're there for nudist bathing or relaxing in a more conventional way, is the tranquillity. It was so quiet. I can't imagine how anyone from a bustling city would react to it. Maybe some would even find it too quiet. The beauty of Holkham. A secret British seaside.

As we drove away from Holkham, Yanny and I talked about the Suffolk resort of Southwold, which I was planning on visiting. Yanny told me how his favourite place to go swimming in the sea in Norfolk was Covehithe, which sits slap bang in between Southwold and Lowestoft.

The contrast between the two resorts couldn't be greater. Southwold is one of the most upper class and beautiful resorts in the UK. When you get off the train in Lowestoft, however, you see nothing but boarded-up buildings, fast-food places and charity shops. The writer W G Sebald, born in Germany but long-term resident of East Anglia, was particularly harsh about Lowestoft in his book *Rings of Saturn*, describing the feeling he felt when he spent time there as one of 'wretchedness'.

'It's great at the moment,' Yanny told me, 'because the poor people in Lowestoft have got a Blue Flag and the rich in Southwold haven't. It's the first time that's ever happened, in however long it is since Blue Flags were invented. In fact they were probably invented by the people of Southwold just to make them look good.'

Blue Flags, it turned out, were actually created in France in 1985 and awarded to beaches meeting sewage and bathing water criteria. In the UK Blue Flags are awarded each year by Keep Britain Tidy in recognition of water quality, safety and cleanliness.

'Whenever we swim at Covehithe,' Yanny continued, 'we swim away from the rich people, towards Lowestoft, because we know the water's cleaner there.' For Yanny, the East Anglian coast was by far the best place for a bracing dip: 'When you're swimming in the sea in Southend, it's not the sea. It's all the excrement that's come out of London. Same with Rhyl, Colwyn Bay, Llandudno: you're just swimming in the Irish Sea. Here there's no doubt you are in the sea. There's nowhere better to swim.'

Yanny explained that to understand Holkham you need to be aware of Walsingham. This tiny village a few miles away occupies a unique place in history as the premier place for pilgrimage in England. Founded at the time of the Crusades when it wasn't possible to visit the Holy Land, English Christians were able to visit this particular version of 'Nazareth' in their own country. Walsingham became the premier shrine to the Virgin Mary and around it grew a large monastery, still visited by more than 300,000 visitors every year. There is nothing religious in this country to rival it. Most kings and queens of history have been there.

'I guess Holkham is God's private beach,' Yanny said, taking another sip of energy drink, and switching on 5 Live.

Wells-next-the-Sea was another beach that had eluded me for far too long. It had eluded many other people too in recent years, being yet another victim of the Beeching Axe; what once would have been a comfortable 30-minute train ride from Norwich would now be a journey lasting three hours and 18 minutes, including two trains and a bus. Wells station, open from 1843 until 1964, is now a second-hand bookshop and pottery. The corn mill which had been adjacent to the station, as with so many buildings by the seaside, is now flats.

We parked in the car park and had barely walked ten feet before we saw a group of musicians singing sea shanties and traditional folk songs on a fish restaurant boat specialising in mussels. We went for a wander to the sound of *Dirty Old Town*.

We walked down a little country lane, passing a house with a double-padlocked front door. 'You know why that is, don't you?' Yanny said. 'They're never there. Needs to be well locked up for when they're in their flats in London.'

People buying up property as second homes is a problem for many seaside towns. Out of season there just aren't people in town, no-one to support local businesses. In many of these seaside towns these second home owners face hostility over what is seen as a privilege for the rich. It's by no means all owners of holiday homes: many spend as much time there as in their permanent places of residence. But to some these seaside homes are part of their investment portfolios or a way of showing off. There is certainly a sense that they are not welcome, the seaside atrophying as the shops find themselves with no customers to sell their goods to whenever it's not the weekend or the summer; no-one sleeping in the beds of the houses.

Seaside towns are in great enough peril without them being empty for large parts of the year. It's the people who live their lives there who suffer as a consequence. People don't come on holiday to places like Wells. There's not enough here for them. Just an amusement arcade and a chip shop and a group of friends singing shanties.

We stopped for a beer in a pub with a flat tiled roof. Travelling around so many seaside resorts I'd had plenty of experience of slipping off for a Kronenbourg in pubs with flat tiled roofs. Yanny and I found a table and talked about our holidays growing up.

'We're all Napoleons in our own homes these days,' he told me. 'People go everywhere by car, check into their rooms and pull up the drawbridge. There used to be something communal about holidays, the coach trips and bed and breakfast where other people join you in the dining room. But now that just seems slightly archaic, that someone else cooks you breakfast while you wait.'

'The big thing that's changed,' Yanny said to me, looking around the room, 'is that pubs don't cater for kids as much as they used to. Once a pub like this would have catered for kids. A ball pool in the corner. Pubs say that since the smoking ban they've become more family friendly, but it's nothing like it used to be. I remember one holiday we had as a family in Southport in Lancashire. All the grown-ups were drinking. I remember being tired, so I crawled under the table to go to sleep. My mum covered me in a blanket, and they carried on drinking. That's what holidays were like. That's the image of our holidays I like to remember.'

Finishing our pints, we headed down to have a look at the beach. As if the Beeching Axe and second-home syndrome weren't enough, Wells-next-the-Sea also had the elements to contend with. The Norfolk coast is almost 100 miles long, and much of that is affected by erosion. Wells-next-the-Sea had a particularly innovative way of tackling this, installing self-cleaning glass flood defences where there was once rotting wood. These defences, paid for by the Environment Agency, were described by the local MP Norman Lamb as 'an asset to the town', the glass allowing for beautiful views of the town and sea.

Not only did Wells suffer from coastal erosion, but it had also been particularly affected by a storm that hit the East of England in January 1953, when 307 people died. Low-lying land was almost completely submerged. Power went off, telephone lines were brought down; Norfolk and Lincolnshire were particularly affected with deaths and the wrecking of buildings and promenades. Wells-next-the-Sea was a particularly newsworthy story, with a 160-ton vessel left washed up on the shore. In Wells they've got marks on the houses to show how high the floods were. You're looking up to the second floor.

'Do you know about Dunwich?' Yanny asked, keen to impart yet more of his local knowledge as we walked on. 'It's the city that fell into the sea. It's a village now. They say that if the wind is in the right direction you can still hear the church bells ring underneath the water. Bollocks of course.'

All the way down the East Anglian coast, there were stories of residents fighting against a similar fate. Peter Boggis was a retired engineer in Southwold, whose house was 302 feet from a rapidly eroding cliff edge. He was fighting his own battle against coastal erosion by dumping thousands of tons of soil to try to 'keep back the sea'. A similar case involved Richard and Anna Hollis, owners of a North Norfolk holiday park who spent £190,000 of their own money 'shoring up the crumbling cliff to save their business'. Michael Kennedy, meanwhile, has been throwing stones and boulders against

Hunstanton cliff for two hours each day, six days a week, for 14 years in a one-man bid to create a tidal barrier and protect it from erosion.

Yanny and I were feeling a bit eroded, too, by this point, so we headed back for the car. The seaside, I realised, a bit like all of us, would possibly be okay if left alone. But nature has a tendency of getting in the way and more often than not at the least convenient time. Coastal towns have had so much to battle with, most notably money and visitor problems, but nothing bigger than nature itself.

CHAPTER SIX

The East Anglian Las Vegas

I've always liked Great Yarmouth. It's not a resort that will ever make it into any of those Sunday supplement lists of seaside resorts to go before you die – this is a town where Manchester United are still sponsored by Sharp – but it has a very real feel of how the seaside used to be.

My sister lives abroad now, and when she came to visit me for a few days in Norwich we decided to go to Great Yarmouth, half an hour away on the train. After a series of are-we-nearly-there-yets from the table next to us, a mum told her kids that Great Yarmouth was 400 miles away, an interesting tactic that seemed to work; after protesting that this would take forever, the group of under-fives, who had been so hyperactive before the train left Norwich station, were suddenly subdued and well behaved. As we got closer they started to anticipate the imminent arrival. 'Is that the sea?' one of them asked.

'It's the sea!' his siblings agreed, all excited. 'We're at the sea! Look, there's the beach!'

What the children were excitedly pointing at was flooded marshland preceding the big 24-hour Asda signifying the train's arrival in Great Yarmouth. But that group of kids was proof that demands are not high; a glimpse of the sea, a bit of sand, maybe even some sunshine is all we want on our holidays and days away. To them the miserable conditions and the fact that it was Great Yarmouth rather than somewhere tropical was irrelevant. In their heads, they could see the sea.

To get to the seafront, whether you've parked or arrived by train, it is likely you will walk down Regent Road. This is the road that makes Great Yarmouth so unmistakably Great Yarmouth. Beyond the Spudulike, a 99p store and a Wetherspoon's is a shop boasting rails of cardigans with embroidered pictures of dogs, sizes up to 5XL, wrapped in polythene to protect them from the rain. Four bath towels were yours for £10. A Jaguar was parked outside the tattoo and body-piercing studio. Prince's Restaurant advertises liver, onions, chips and peas for £5.65. A shop called Good Times has closed down, the irony not lost to anyone within earshot of the busker on the corner, playing *My Old Man's A Dustman*, giving the tune its own unique Norfolk slant. There was no-one around to put money in his upturned flat cap.

At the bottom of the road is the T-junction with the Esplanade. The Brittania Pier has billboards advertising forthcoming events: Joe Pasquale, Roy 'Chubby' Brown, Cannon and Ball. But on closer inspection all of these dates had passed six months previously: The Chuckle Brothers and Derek Acorah had been and gone during the summer season. The only attractions advertised for the near future were The Osmonds and Gareth Gates in *Boogie Nights*, also featuring Chico, Andy Abraham and Shane Ritchie Junior.

As we walked away from the pier to what is known as the Golden Mile, a road parallel to the seafront, I wondered whether the Britannia Pier had left these boards up deliberately because they had nothing to replace them with. Certainly, nothing that would evoke that era so synonymous with the town and celebrated by generations holidaying in Great Yarmouth, a place of doughnuts, slot machines and entertainment on the pier. If they took the names of the likes of Joe Pasquale down it could destroy the town's soul.

The boards were clear indications that it was a town looking backwards rather than forwards, memories of a great past. The Chuckle Brothers and Cannon and Ball won't be around forever, they are the last of that lineage – a kind of entertainer that would never be replaced. As retirement looms for the last of the pier entertainers, an era ends in Great Yarmouth. The billboards are like plaques, honouring something treasured and loved, like all names on the benches in memoriam.

In the 1960s, hordes of tourists descended upon Great Yarmouth every summer. The main reason was because it was accessible and there was a sandy beach – what more could anyone desire? By the end of that decade, though, Mods and Rockers started to cause a problem. Although these kinds of clashes were more commonly associated with Brighton and Margate, Yarmouth also suffered several incidents of fighting. The seaside had started to become dangerous; what was once a vibrant, prosperous and thriving seaside town was starting to decline. Now it was little more than a collection of arcades, a branch of Greggs, and people wheelbarrowing their gold to sell.

This was the closest I'd come to the widely regarded dirty seaside town: out of season, raining and deserted, it was a line-up of pub, amusement arcade, pub, arcade, pub, and barely a person in any. Walking down the Golden Mile we passed the once great Empire Theatre, now a nightclub premises to let. Then, after a row of steak houses and cafés, we hit the amusement arcades.

One arcade played the theme tune to *Only Fools and Horses*; the Trevor Francis tracksuits evoked in the lyrics reminiscent of the merchandise for sale in the shops on Regent Road. The song was interrupted by a recorded voice enticing passers-by inside: '£70 jackpots! That's smackers in your pocket, tax free to do whatever you want with. Stick that in your pipe and smoke it, Alistair Darling!'

It had been two and a half years since Alistair Darling was Chancellor of the Exchequer, so you pity the people who have been hearing this voiceover for possibly half a decade. Just as notable a continuity error was the blasting out of *School's Out* by Alice Cooper, encouraging kids that, as it was the holidays, they should come and play in the arcades.

Clearly these messages had been recorded several years ago with the intention of being used for a couple of months.

Like so many things in Great Yarmouth they had either been forgotten, unnoticed, or no-one could be bothered to right the wrongs. 'Win 500 dollareenies,' another message continued, before trying to lure the more suggestive menfolk of Great Yarmouth with this message: 'Lads. Getting earache off the old dear? Then stop her nagging and prove your love by winning her a big fluffy teddy bear.' The prizes on offer are listed, before ending with, 'That'll keep the old ball and chain happy for a while.' To list the number of things wrong with that single statement would take several pages of A4. In one of the cafés on the Golden Mile a local radio station was playing a 'Guess The Year' competition. After the last half an hour I'd experienced it was hard even to guess the decade.

My sister and I used to love amusement arcades when we were little. Fifty pence would last us a whole day, whether it was day trips to Cleethorpes or when we were on holiday in Scarborough, and further along the coast when we'd go to Whitby and Robin Hood's Bay. Now, with computer consoles, kids sit down with a universe on the television screen, rendering the imagination a long-forgotten middleman. As fondly as I remember the arcades, I also remember the rocks on the beach at Robin Hood's Bay. I'm so glad we had all those afternoons on the rocks, the whole afternoon in front of us. We would play there for hours, my sister and me. We'd create a whole universe.

Karen and I had both saved our 2p pieces, like we did in the old days, and set about the seafront parade, where arcades included Goldrush, Caesar's Fun Palace, Atlantis, Mint, Silver Stripper and Golden Nugget. The sight of them made us both genuinely excited: Great Yarmouth was our Vegas. I remember our mum once telling us how much our granddad used to love the arcades. He'd look for money on the road as he was walking along the seafront so that it was someone else's money he was spending. This love for coin pusher machines was clearly something that ran in the family.

Karen had always been luckier than me on the arcades. Certainly less impatient. Whenever we played, as my pocket of coins ran out, the jingles of success would be heard as coins cascaded. Then she'd sweep them into her cupped hand and put all her winnings into her bum bag, for that brief part of the early 1990s when bum bags were acceptable to wear.

This time it was different. The gambling gods of Great Yarmouth were punishing Karen for moving abroad to landlocked Switzerland; her Midas touch had deserted her, being so far from the sea. She was soon at the change booth, exchanging her hard-earned real-life money for 2p pieces. Meanwhile, I was trying out a new method, which I had read about online. The usual technique is to put one coin in, watch it drop, then wait to see the result before inserting the next 2p. Instead, I was going nuclear. I put a handful of coins in, one after another, quick-fire. They cascaded down and soon there was the unmistakable sound of winning, the tray at the bottom filling with 2p pieces. Who would have thought it could be so exciting to win 78p?

I was intrigued as to what it was that Karen and I found so compelling about the coin pushers. This led me to getting in touch with Kenny Marshall, a man who collected arcade machines and had written articles about his love for them. He, like Karen and I, was particularly fond of the coin pushers. I sent Kenny a message explaining that I was fascinated by his collection, and would it be okay to ask him more about his machines?

'My early memories of amusement arcades dates back to around 1975 when I was 11 years old, in Pitlochry, Perthshire,' Kenny replied to me over email. 'In those days the arcade was not much more than a large wooden shack with an elderly couple that owned it who lived round the back in a caravan. Machines that stick out in my mind were an old Steer-A-Coin machine where if you were extremely good your coin would be returned if you were able to complete the 'car course'! The pushers were my always favourites though.'

Kenny explained that the total number of machines he has owned, although not all at one time, was perhaps 70. At its biggest the collection would have probably comprised about 23 machines in his garage. 'My first machine was a £25 jackpot fruit machine, quite an old type, followed by two or three other fruit machines. Then 13 quiz machines, one large food vending machine and two video games. I think my first pusher would slot in about here – it was a single player pusher called *Jungle Treasure* which I drove down to Leeds to collect. Around then I also owned seven one armed bandits all in varying degrees of condition.' Kenny's list went on and on; I didn't have a clue what most of it meant. 'Tap-a-win. Tooty Fruity. Cromputer Win. Bell-fruit wall-mounted penny cascade type machine. Tipper Win. A Rock-Ola jukebox. Obviously there were umpteen pushers and one home-made pusher which I built from nothing myself.'

The words Kenny listed in my inbox conjured up a bygone age. I could picture a freckle-faced ten-year-old Perthshire boy with a glass bottle of Irn Bru he was drinking through a straw, putting his pocket money into these machines, a hobby gradually becoming an obsession until his double garages were so full you could barely open the doors.

I was interested to know how profitable coin pusher machines were. Astonishingly, according to Kenny, the pushers can be responsible for up to 50 per cent of a seaside amusement arcade's revenue. On a good day they are capable of taking in hundreds of pounds. In recent years a combination of the decline of the British seaside holiday and the development in home gaming consoles means that arcades aren't making anything like the amount of money they did in the 1970s and 80s.

Some say perhaps this decline is a good thing; seaside amusement arcades should die out, they would be no loss, they breed gambling and greed and they are unpleasant places for children to spend their time. Away from where Karen and I had been playing the penny pusher machines sat the more sinister part of the amusement arcade. Roped off with a different coloured carpet, this was where the fruit machines stand proud, with people playing on them with the concentration of surgeons. These people weren't here for fun.

Arcades are often perceived as glamorising gambling to children, it's what gives them their first taste of the potential of prizes, and from that moment on a habit can be formed. However, there is also another view. There are others who say that arcades are the perfect antidote to gambling and that they have positive effects on the psyche of children, who go in there at a young age to grab a stuffed Eeyore on the claw machine or to play on the *Bob the Builder* and *Thomas the Tank Engine* rides. At an early age the noises of the arcade and an understanding of winning and losing become indoctrinated into the brain.

Of course, there are similarities with the high-end casinos; the mesmerising flow of the arcades, the music jingling like dollar signs, the sense of every machine about to pay out, a cash win imminent. But these 2p pushers could almost be said to epitomise the right way to gamble. Only putting in what you can afford to lose, never walking away with a big dent in your wallet; a good way to put children off the idea of gambling, that the certainty that the 'house' always wins is as engrained a rule as that your pet rabbit will die. Deal with it.

Owners and fans of amusement arcades would argue that they provide an important role, that without them the alternatives are harder forms of gambling: betting shops and casinos. Getting rid of amusement arcades is not the way to address problem gambling.

I asked Kenny if he could take me around an amusement arcade one day so I could see his techniques, get to know his methods. I had long envied people who made a living by playing fruit and quiz machines. I wanted to learn if there was a knack, or if it was pure luck. Unfortunately Kenny, wasn't keen to meet a stranger and escort him round a variety of seaside amusement arcades, and who can blame him? But he did answer the question that burns inside all of us who have played the penny pushers. Is there a knack? Can we learn the secret and quit our jobs?

'I think it is a self-taught thing after many, many years of experience playing them,' Kenny concluded. 'You get to know when the time is right to play. As a youngster I seldom got it right or if I did I seldom kept what I won, I used to play it back in the hope of winning more but ended up losing in the end. Now I am older and very much wiser. I just stay clear of some machines because you can tell by their design that it will be extremely hard to win from them. I don't think it would be fair to name particular types. I must confess I don't always get it right but without appearing conceited I think it would be fair to say 95 per cent of the time I do.'

Kenny explained how different machines had different characteristics: 'the older machines were certainly a lot easier to win from than the present day ones. In my opinion, pushers which were built in the mid-to-late eighties were a lot easier to win from. Changing the size of the ten pence coin in 1992 was a big disadvantage – it is much lighter and as such it does make winning harder. So the older the machine I can find to play the better.'

So how much could an expert like Kenny win on one of these machines? 'My maximum winnings ever in a day from playing pushers was around £80 at the Links Market, an annual fair in Kirkcaldy, Fife. Next to this I have probably made around £20 to £25 on a good day in Blackpool in the eighties.'

I was happy with the 78p that was weighing down my pocket, soon to be reinvested and inevitably lost.

I had never been particularly interested in arcade games growing up. In the 1980s, when kids across the world were skipping school to play on arcade machines, I was diligently doing my maths homework, pocket money safely in my moneybox. But I was in the minority: millions loved the arcades. In 1978, when *Space Invaders* was released in Japan it caused a national shortage of 100 yen coins, meaning more had to be manufactured. Soon games like *Donkey Kong*, *Frogger*, *Mario Bros.*, *Paperboy* and *Street Fighter* were appearing in amusement arcades, and so began a lifetime of gaming for many.

I talked to my friend Tim, a writer and computer games obsessive, about this phenomenon. Tim had been obsessed with arcades since he was a schoolboy growing up in

Portishead. He remembered the loss of seaside arcades in the same way many people feel about the slow disappearance of independent record stores and bookshops in the face of the internet. He has over a thousand arcade games stored on his laptop, which he can play for free whenever he likes.

'I remember in Paul McCartney's autobiography,' he told me when we met in the pub one evening, 'he said they'd hear somebody on the other side of Liverpool knew a chord they couldn't play, like E13, and they'd have to catch two buses to go and meet the guy to learn it, or they'd get to know a guy who had an LP of an amazing band from the US, and they'd all pile into his bedroom to listen to it. It built a community. You got to know like-minded people. Seaside arcades used to be like that.'

Tim explained how a group of friends would save up and then get the bus to Weston-super-Mare together: 'On the way you'd be deciding what games you'd play on when you arrived. Sometimes there'd be a new machine in the arcade, sometimes you'd walk in and there'd be this guy chain-smoking, cruising through *Wonderboy* without losing a life. I remember seeing a guy playing *Pac-Land* (the side-scrolling 'platformer' sequel to *Pac-Man*). He made Pac-Man jump over a fire hydrant then turn around, he *pushed the fire hydrant aside*, and suddenly Pac-Man was wearing a hard hat and ghosts that fell on him didn't hurt him. That was my E13 chord.'

Tim and his fellow gamers were the 1980s equivalent of Paul McCartney and the aspiring musicians on Merseyside. 'Back then, you learned secrets from watching other gamers. Now you can just go on gaming websites and it's all there, everything you'd ever want to know. Back then, knowledge was at a premium. There was an inner circle, and if you knew the secret code that made Shang Tsung turn his opponent into a baby on *Mortal Kombat 3*, you could draw a crowd.'

Tim said he still associated the smell of fag smoke and the beeps and jingles of video games with feeling very, very safe and at home.

'Many people didn't play, they just watched. Often word would spread around at how to get to the next level. Someone would reach a new part of the game and people would rush over to see what was happening. It was very voyeuristic, a big part of people's lives.'

His favourite arcades were in Weston-super-Mare. The Grand Pier there describes itself as 'the ultimate indoor theme park', with 4D cinema, a ghost train, helter skelter, dodgems, Formula 1 simulators and over 500 fruit machines just on that one pier. 'Three storeys of moving floors, mirrors and mayhem.' It also boasts Britain's smallest rollercoaster, developed from a robotic arm used in automated car plants, which thrashes its two passengers at high velocity high above the arcade machines. The ride swings passengers around and around, up and down and upside down. Following the 2008 fire on the pier, which completely destroyed the pavilion, Weston-super-Mare's pier was rebuilt at a cost of £39 million and reopened on 23 October 2010. It seemed the polar opposite from where Karen and I were stood in Great Yarmouth.

Tim, like Kenny, was pretty sceptical about the future of seaside arcades, saying he knew for certain the best days had gone for good. 'Society is different nowadays,' Kenny had told me. 'Some resorts, although by no means all, are not so safe as they were when I was young. It's not just safety, though, it's as simple as this: I don't think the modern machines are as good as the old ones. There's something missing for me, and I don't think it's just because I am getting older. Home video games and consoles certainly can't be helping the arcades either. I guess there must be a lot less video games played in arcades than when I was growing up.'

In case the general decline of seaside towns and the rise in home gaming wasn't enough, government proposals have threatened to make life even tougher, replacing VAT with Machine Games Duty. In 2011, Derek Petrie of BACTA, which represents the British Amusement Industry, said, 'We have seen over 200 amusement arcades close in the past two years, many of them small family-run businesses. While the Government is busy promoting UK seaside tourism with one hand, the Treasury seems intent on taking it away with the other.'

The smoking ban hasn't helped either, and all in all the future is not too promising. There are around 500 amusement arcades left in the UK, and most of them are living on the edge. As my sister and I walked along Great Yarmouth seafront with almost every square inch of every amusement arcade to ourselves, this not only felt all too apparent, but also a shame. We'd had fun splatting moles with a plastic hammer, playing on the Addams Family pinball and, most importantly, diligently putting 2p pieces down a chute. In the end we lost about £3 each. Although neither of us drive Rolls-Royces, we could afford to lose that kind of money. It was an enjoyable way to spend a stress-free afternoon.

Karen and I didn't stay in Yarmouth for long after we left the arcades. The pier was closed and even some chip shops had shut up for the winter. The previous year the Yarmouth amusement arcades had been put up for sale but were saved after being bought by a specialist restructuring, recovery and insolvency firm. Ah, the romance of the seaside.

CHAPTER SEVEN

The Zimmer Frame Simulator

Southwold and Great Yarmouth might have been separated by less than 20 miles of East Anglian coastline, but the contrast between the two resorts could not have been sharper. Some dismiss Southwold as being too posh; it is often dubbed 'Chelsea-by-the-Sea', and Suzy's Café on the seafront does sell prawn sandwiches and elderflower pressé and ginger beer.

One of the town's notable fans is Michael Palin, who used to go on holiday there when he was little and met his wife there. When visiting Southwold to reopen the cinema he described it as 'a town full of harmony and architectural features that go together beautifully and the fact that is still here is wonderful'. Palin isn't the only fan of the area. Actors including Geoffrey Palmer, Rowan Atkinson and Bill Nighy are all reported to have beach huts in Southwold. That's one hell of a boules team.

When I told people I was writing this book, many suggested I visit Southwold to experience its esoteric, charming, unique pier. Built in 1900, it was originally 810 feet long but after several incidents and accidents, most notably during the Second World War, it was reduced to a mere 60 feet. In 2005 new management arrived, making intriguing improvements to what is now largely known as 'the best loved and truly 21st-century pier in the country', restored to be close to its original length.

On arriving I immediately knew it was my kind of place. It was a sunny day, the first for what seemed like months. I'd gone out without my coat on. It's always an exciting moment when you leave it on its peg. A man in a bobble hat popped into the famous Sailors' Reading Room, built as a refuge for sailors and fishermen, now known locally as a quiet spot to go through the papers with a pot of tea, have a nice sit down.

The main attraction, for me, was the *Under the Pier* exhibition. This was a series of handmade coin-operated arcade machines, lovingly constructed and tucked away in a room at the end of the pier. It was a world away from the roped-off gambling sections of Great Yarmouth's amusement arcades.

The first machine I used was called The Chiropodist, a doll of a female chiropodist in a white coat with glasses, in a cage. You have to take your shoes off and put your foot in a hole in the cage. The doll reaches down and suddenly you get the most eerie sensation of pipe-cleaner fingers touching your foot. It's so, so creepy. It's unpleasant. I let out

an *'Eurgh!'* as a dad and his two boys were watching. That's
the problem with this exhibition: whenever you play on
anything people will watch you. It's captivating, no-one has
ever seen anything like this. I'm not someone who would
ever go on arcade machines or play on consoles – I'm not
very good at that kind of thing – but this exhibition was so
much more than that. I just found myself wanting to have a
go on as many machines as possible.

Next I played on Pet or Meat. You have to wind up
a handle, press a button and then an arrow on a roulette
wheel stops, determining whether the little lamb you saw in
the box in front of you will remain a family pet or become
a family dinner. I span and, almost inevitably, the arrow
landed on meat. The happy, smiling, clay model family with
the lamb revolved, revealing the son and daughter banging
their knives and forks on the dinner table, the dad carving
the lamb and the mum with two steaks on her fork. It's
gruesome. It's so over the top and upsetting but somehow
so, so funny: again, unlike anything you would ever expect
to experience on a pier.

A machine called Walking the Dog involved standing
on a treadmill, taking hold of a dog's lead. The dog's head
spins, he turns to you and smiles, and then you're off, with a
video projection in front of you as he simulates scampering
off down Southwold High Street. Occasionally you have
to pull on the lead to take your dog away from trees and
lampposts. Your dog can even fall in love. There's a screen
at the dog's eye level where you can see everything from
the dog's perspective. It actually felt comforting. As with
everything else at the exhibition it was cheap to play and the

game lasted a long time. What else can you get enjoyment from using just two 20p coins?

Finally, I played on a game where you have to cross the road with a Zimmer frame, a game inspired by Southwold's elderly population. The Zimmer Frame Simulator involved having to try and cross a computer-simulated four-lane motorway while standing on a platform holding on to a Zimmer frame. There are three difficulty settings for the game – aged 80 (easy), aged 90 (medium) and aged 100 (difficult). I don't normally play this kind of thing but I just felt desperate to have a go.

'You have fewer inhibitions when on a pier,' the arcade's designer and engineer, Tim Hunkin, explained to me later, when I emailed him to tell him how much I loved his exhibition. It's exactly the way I felt; I hate people looking at me normally, but holding a Zimmer frame, guiding an old lady across the road over four lines of traffic to get to a dance hall, I didn't mind that most eyes in the small room were watching my attempt. Players get to have two practice goes, both of which I failed. I was hit by a car and when that happens you see on the screen a toppled-over Zimmer frame, sirens blare out, an ambulance arrives, two paramedics get out, draw a white chalk line and put cones around the incident while traffic builds up, tooting their horns. You genuinely feel as if you're responsible for an old lady's death.

When it was my turn to play for real, when it explicitly tells you that this is your only chance, if you don't get across you have failed, I was determined to get across. Three boys were watching me as I gripped hard on the Zimmer frame. I was so careful, concentrating fully, and I did it. I got her there. I won. The boys cheered and our reward at the end of the simulator was to see the computerised ballroom on the screen and my old lady dancing around the ballroom. I was euphoric, even though it was so horrible. The game was so surreal and weird, it was as if I wasn't at a seaside, on a pier, in Southwold, but in a different universe, one where the only thing that mattered was the welfare of this doddery old lady.

'My taste is for stuff that is a bit tacky and decaying but is also a bit sad,' Tim Hunkin told me later. 'Generally I have a love–hate relationship with Southwold. It can be appallingly snobbish, mainly as a result of having so many second-home owners, but it also has charm. The lack of vandalism is particularly useful to me; my arcade couldn't survive unattended in many other seaside piers.'

Under the Pier is Hunkin's ongoing obsession. He makes a new machine for it every year, with the occasional help of his sister. The delight on people's faces when they entered the *Under the Pier* show was something I hadn't seen once at the other seaside arcades I had been to; there was such enjoyment in that room, a genuine buzz. Locals and holidaymakers all enjoying arcades such as the Auto Frisk machine, with its rubber gloves, simulating what it's like to be frisked. Everyone was having a go, every machine was being used, people were squealing with delight whether they were playing themselves or just observing their friends, family or strangers.

Hunkin's exhibition had played a large part in Southwold's transformation into one of the most significant resorts and the most enjoyable places to visit. He is clearly a man with a lot of affection for seaside towns and is optimistic about their future: 'I'm keen to see the resorts reinvent themselves. I think piers will survive, because people won't suddenly stop enjoying trips to the seaside.' Yet again the involvement of an eccentric had changed a seaside town for the better.

Standing on Southwold Pier looking south, the eye is drawn along the seafront and the town's promenade. Nestled in the centre, at the heart of the town, is its lighthouse: rather than sitting out at sea on a rocky outcrop, Southwold's tower pokes its head out of the skyline, nestled among the second homes and coffee shops.

I've always been fascinated by lighthouses. When I was teaching up in Aberdeen I had driven past a sign for the Museum of Scottish Lighthouses, on the site of the first lighthouse built on mainland Scotland. There is something intriguing about the life of a lighthouse keeper. The isolation, the repetition, was baffling and alluring; so I parked up, wandered in and a guided tour was just starting.

Our guide, a lovely polite boy who can barely have been a toddler when the last lighthouse keeper packed up his suitcase and walked down the spiral staircase for the final time, told us that the first lighthouse in Scotland was built in 1794 by Robert Stevenson and his stepfather, Thomas Smith.

Stevenson was then involved with the building of at least 15 major lighthouses. His son Alan became his apprentice, and it was he who designed Skerryvore, considered by many to be the world's most beautiful lighthouse. Robert Stevenson's two other sons, David and Thomas, also worked with lighthouses. Thomas, father of author Robert Louis Stevenson, author of *Treasure Island*, was particularly fascinated by optics, and as a consequence Scottish lights became the most powerful and versatile in the world. The family lighthouse business carried on for further generations, a Russian doll of Stevensons, most recently with David Alan Stevenson, who died in 1971, considered to be one of the world's foremost experts on the history of lighthouses.

Our guide that day took us up to the viewing platform to see the lenses on display. These lenses made me realise the magnitude of what was involved in working on a lighthouse, just a few people in charge of such overpowering objects. Being a keeper must have been a scary job.

On the stairs near the café were photographs by Keith Allardyce, who had realised long in advance that by the end of the 20th century every lighthouse would be unmanned. In the late 1970s and late 90s he set out to make photographic records of what life in the lighthouse was like. He visited 80 lighthouses, from the Isle of Man to Shetland, photographing cliffs, wives, families and dogs for an exhibition called *At Scotland's Edge*. Most of all it was just keepers at work in the lighthouse, a tradition that after centuries was coming to an end. The last lighthouse in the UK was automated in 1998, I learned – North Foreland Lighthouse, Kent. One of the principal uses since automation is as a base for satellite communication, particularly GPS. It is a long time since they have been manned by a man with a big white beard and yellow sou'wester.

Ever since that visit to Scotland, I'd been keen to find out more about lighthouses and their keepers. I found an email address for the Association of Lighthouse Keepers and it turned out that Gerry, the organisation's archivist and co-founder, lived in the Suffolk town of Bungay, just a short drive from Southwold. By chance he lived a few roads down from my friends Luke and Sally, whom I was going to go to see anyway. So not only would I be able to meet the person who I thought could answer all the questions I had about lighthouses, I could go round to theirs for my tea afterwards.

I met Gerry in a Bungay pub, where we spent a hugely enjoyable afternoon. He was a tall, thin man, who had been hard to identify at first because I was expecting someone wearing a bright yellow sou'wester, big bushy beard and binoculars round his neck. I had mythologised lighthouse keepers as though they slew dragons or rode seahorses. He was clean-shaven, with spectacles and a light jacket. I was excruciatingly disappointed. Despite this setback I decided I'd still talk to him. I'm very gracious like that.

Gerry's 28-year career as a lighthouse keeper had its origins in Southwold. He told me how he had left school in 1970, and gone to study mechanical engineering in London. He had some private funds so took six months off. During this time, his dad took over a fishing tackle shop in Southwold. While he was refurbishing the premises, Gerry looked around the front part of the shop, an empty room other than a chest of drawers, which he opened and found a 1954 careers encyclopaedia which fell open at 'lighthouse keeper'.

'Talk about fate taking your hand!' Gerry said. 'I decided there and then to become a keeper.' Traditionally lighthouse keepers were born rather than recruited; father and son, father and son. But in the mid-20th century that died out and there were as many trades and professions as there were lighthouse keepers, with people like Gerry considering it a viable career option. Often people were stuck, living lives of not belonging anywhere, and ended up working in a lighthouse. The most surprising thing to learn was that rather than working in a lighthouse, you were sent from place to place, rarely given time to settle. To talk to Gerry about the lighthouses he had worked on was to get a guided tour of the coast of the UK.

'In the first year you're on probation. Sent round different lighthouses in your district. I had East Cowes district. The jurisdiction was from Dungeness to Portland Bill, and included the Channel Islands. I'd never been to the Channel Islands. You get a letter through the post, get your air tickets, it's quite an adventure.'

Gerry joined the service at the age of 21. In 28 years he covered 18 different stations, from Flanborough Head down to the west coast of Wales and all points in between.

'I was particularly fond of Flat Holm,' he told me. 'It's near the Bristol Channel, between Cardiff and Weston-super-Mare. It's a 60-acre island; the other two keepers and I had the complete run of the place. The best thing about Flat Holm was we were transported there by helicopter.'

I was really struggling to get to grips with a lighthouse keeper who wasn't fictional. I didn't want to ask him questions that could have come from a primary school kid.

But I was still slightly confused and wanted to know about the day-to-day life. I asked him to try and break down the lighthouse keeper's life.

'Let's take Beachy Head as an example,' he told me. 'There were three keepers there. You'd spend two months at sea. When you were there you stayed there. Your whole life was in there. You stay indoors and that's it. Self-imposed exile. It was like nice prison. Every month a boat would come out as relief and the keepers would change over and you'd get to go home. When the helicopters came in the rota patterns changed to a month on, a month off: 28 days at sea, 28 days at home.'

This is where the difficulties lay. Lighthouse keepers were thrown together with other work colleagues. They couldn't go anywhere, there was no escape. If they really didn't like someone they could apply for a transfer, but that rarely happened. I think I'd have coped well as a lighthouse keeper. It sounded a little bit like temping. My experience at Anglia Windows and Norwich Union would have been invaluable, and I liked the idea of looking out at the waves. It would be good to have a job with a view.

Talking to Gerry, there wasn't the sense of adventure or peril I had expected: he loved Flat Holm for its fitted carpets, central heating and double glazing. After Flat Holm he was transferred to The Needles, where he worked for twelve and a half years – the longest a keeper had ever been there – and he served it all the way through to its automation in 1998.

'It was a bit of a tourist spot,' Gerry remembered. 'There were always yachts going past, Alum Bay is not far with its chair lift and coloured sand. We had visitors throughout the year. People would drop in; canoeists, swimmers, tourists. There'd be a knock at the door downstairs, you'd trot down to answer it and someone would say "Ooh can we have a look around?" so you'd make them a cup of tea. This is something you couldn't do at any other towers like at Beachy Head because the access was so bad. For anyone who asked what a typical lighthouse was like, I would suggest The Needles. The lighthouses you see in fiction are likely to be based on The Needles. But even then you lived on the station. We had a coal fire and Raeburn in the kitchen. It was very much a traditional tower. Curved doors, curved cupboards, curved bunks.'

I was fascinated by what occupied Gerry's time on the lighthouse when he wasn't on shift. At Christmas, they'd still put out tinsel and a tree, make the most of it. As for the rest of the year, Gerry told me keeping busy with hobbies was the most important part of being a lighthouse keeper. Many took great pride in what they did in their spare time. People did woodwork; one keeper used to make model farm carts with bespoke wheels in tiny detail. One keeper used to build models of lighthouses inside navigational lamps. Gerry was interested in motorcycles.

'I used to take parts out there, gearboxes, carburettors; I used to draw, read, write. I ran a magazine for nine and a half years,' he told me, putting his carrier bag on the table and presenting me with a slim publication entitled *Association of Lighthouse Keepers*. 'Something you are going away with,' he said, beaming a smile.

Gerry also read avidly when on the lighthouses, three books going at once. He read all of Dickens, the Bible cover to cover, the complete works of Shakespeare. He explained that the actual keeping was a fairly mundane job. One of his happiest memories of his time as a keeper was when he worked in a lighthouse that had a postbox at the end of the driveway. So much of a lighthouse keeper's life involved writing letters, at times you would spend weeks waiting to send off mail, so to have a postbox so close was a real luxury.

The only reason they employed keepers was because all the equipment had to be operated by hand, so with automation – microchips taking over the duties of the keeper – so many were made redundant. Contrary to common belief, part of their duties was never to keep a vigilant watch for lifesaving purposes. Their remit was to look after the equipment on board, to be an aid to navigation, to clean, tidy, service, change oil filters. He really seemed to have embraced the isolation of the job.

'There was never isolation,' he quickly corrected me. 'Just solitude. Never isolation.'

I asked Gerry about the process of automation. I'd been nervous about asking this; I felt as if I was saying, 'How did your childhood dog die?' But I was pleasantly surprised at Gerry's non-Luddite response. I completely expected him to be seething towards the machines that had cruelly robbed him of his livelihood. Before I met Gerry, I'd have expected him to be a *'Why do we need clocks? There was nothing wrong with sundials'* type of person. But instead he just shrugged his shoulders and seemed fine about it. The world moves and you have to try your best to keep up with it. Even if you are a retired lighthouse keeper.

I asked Gerry how far off from reality the fictionalised version of lighthouses I'd seen on TV and in books really was.

'Oh, you mean sou'wester, rollneck sweater,' Gerry laughed. 'Miles away. Occasionally you'd have to dress up in your uniform with your brass buttons but that was only on special occasions. You just wore the same thing most days. The only place to dry anything would be the engine room, which was full of diesel fumes. The only place you could have a wash would be in a plastic bowl or in the sink. When the other keepers were asleep it was your opportunity to have a strip-down wash, stand in a plastic bowl. The popular image is fairly wide of the mark, an old boy with a bushy white Captain Birdseye beard.'

'With a dog stealing a string of sausages from the butchers,' I added, mainly because I loved watching *Portland Bill* when I was little. There was a sense of complete enjoyment in Gerry as he was recounting these tales from the lighthouses, his stories from the seaside. He seemed to have very happy memories from his time as a keeper.

Back on Southwold Pier, my attention was drawn from the lighthouse on the skyline to the rail I had been leaning on. Rather than a simple, wooden frame, I noticed that it was covered in commemorative plaques: a banister of memories around Southwold Pier. They provided a history of the people who had walked along the wooden planks, the North Sea visible between the gaps underneath the wobbly floorboards.

The plaques evoke so many memories that you cannot help but feel humbled by them. To read every single one of them would take weeks, there are thousands, but I spent a long time exploring them, lives contained within a thumbnail. Each piece of brass takes you to a different place, evoking feelings only the finest literature or cinema could ever get close to. Some of the dedications on the plaques are unbearably sad, but at the same time life affirming, enriching. The seaside meant so much to these names, these families, the people who had commissioned the plaques. They were places of happiness, contentment, lives well lived:

> *Pooh and Piglet, with love from all of us on your wedding day. June 22nd 2002. Happy days.*
>
> *In memory of Jerry Dobson who for 40 years loved the pier and the town.*
>
> *Southwold, better than Prozac, Mike and Helen Green.*
>
> *Blackberry and Treacle. Two dear cats.*
>
> *Still here. Still in love with Southwold and each other. Tim and Gillian McArtney. 1981–2002.*
>
> *James and Georgina Cooper enjoyed many gin and tonics here.*

This continued over thousands and thousands of plaques. If you put all of the small brass dedications that were at the most 10 centimetres wide end to end, you would reach Aberdeen or Hawaii or Neptune, certainly somewhere a long, long way from Suffolk. The messages were so beautiful and heartfelt. I did what many people do when confronted with emotions. I went back inside to play on the games in the arcade.

CHAPTER EIGHT

The Essex Rainbow

As I explored the seaside resorts of the East Anglian coast, I decided I'd had enough treats; discovering secret beaches, meeting a retired lighthouse keeper, playing Whack-a-Mole in the arcades and all those cones of chips. It was time to go to Essex.

It was horrible weather. I knew it as soon as my alarm went off at 7am. 'You're not going to like what you'll see when you open the curtains,' the beep beep beeps seemed to be telling me as I hammered the palm of my hand down on *Snooze*. It was one of those mornings where, even if you were in a soundproof room with no windows, you'd be able to tell it was a bit grim outside. Around 95 per cent of our brain is used to detect drizzle.

As I left the house and walked to Norwich train station, fully formed puddles were falling from the sky. This weather seemed somehow appropriate. I'd decided to have a look at the seaside's dark underbelly, find out what lurks beneath the sand, within the chip wrappings. Seaside resorts can be dangerous places, with their red flags and warning signs and high tides. They can seem unappealing too: pollution, rotting piers, crime, drugs, social deprivation and all those party political conferences.

I wanted to find out the problems, the negative aspects, the things the guidebooks don't tell you. According to a case study carried out by Sheffield Hallam University in 2008, 26 of the 37 principal seaside towns have greater overall deprivation than the national average: 31 have greater unemployment; and 28 have greater health and disability deprivation than the English average.

Jaywick Sands in Essex is a town that has suffered more than most. In fact, it is regarded as the most run-down seaside resort in the UK. A 2010 government report, taking into account income, employment, health, disability, crime and living standards, concluded that Jaywick was at the bottom of the deprivation table. It was a 2011 article in the *Guardian* that had alerted me to Jaywick: 'the area is relatively isolated and the properties have deteriorated', the article claimed. 'A total of 62 per cent of working age residents receive benefits, compared with the national average of 15 per cent.'

The train was taking me to Clacton-on-Sea, the nearest station stop to Jaywick Sands. From there I planned to walk around the coast to Jaywick. I half expected that when I got there, the whole town would be jumping up and down on the bonnet of a Nissan Sunny.

As my train took me south, I took out a selection of articles I'd printed out about the state of the British seaside. It didn't make for happy reading and it seemed almost indelicate to go and spend time somewhere that had already been written about in such negative terms. Destruction and dereliction are sadly a common theme in seaside towns across the country. In 2007, the Rhyl funfair was demolished to make way for Ocean Plaza: a supermarket, hotel and flats. The Great Yarmouth rollercoaster has to be examined on a daily basis by staff to make sure it is safe to run. Seaside resorts are often increasingly dangerous places, not just with the falling-apart funfairs, but on a social level.

The grim statistics continued as my train rumbled on. If you mention the seaside to somebody it is just as likely that their response will be relating to the negative reports like the ones in front of me as to a donkey ride or bucket and spade. In seaside towns the average rate of personal insolvencies is around one third higher than the national average. Official figures from the Department for Education show that Blackpool has 74.8 conceptions per 1,000 girls aged 15 to 17, compared with a national average of 42.6. Another place often mentioned when seaside deprivation is talked about is Weston-super-Mare, which is home to around 11 per cent of drug rehabilitation centres in the UK. This had consequences; local police reported that people dropping out of the programme 'spawned a mini-crime wave'.

One theory is that this is attributed to a 'sense of detachment' young people experience in seaside towns. This results in a 'suspension of reality', which encourages casual sex and a lack of responsibility for the consequences of actions. Clacton Pier has seen young people killed after jumping overboard, and in recent years has fought against 'tombstoning' – an activity involving jumping down into the water from a steep drop.

I put down these grim statistics and encounters I was reading about, and turned to see if social media might offer me a more positive view. At the start of my journey from Norwich I had posted on Twitter that I was heading to Clacton-on-Sea that morning. Never have I received so many responses, and none were filling me with optimism for my visit: 'Stop while you have the chance! It took me 19 years to get out!' read one; 'I was there in Feb. Took my boyfriend for a romantic break. Big mistake', recalled another. The most succinct message of them all simply said, 'Why?'

The first thing I noticed as I got off the train at Clacton was a broken umbrella in the dustbin outside the station. The winds that had been rattling the windows of our train were in Clacton too, like an unwelcome guest at Christmas, eating all the mince pies. It was raining hard as it had been in Norwich, and I headed into town with my hat on, hands thrust deep in my pockets.

The first two buildings you see in Clacton are an estate agent called Moving Places and a funeral directors, presenting you with the two recommendations of how best to get out of the town. I walked past closed-down shops, amusement arcades and a Wimpy. Even the pigeons looked a bit sad. There was a fountain, which had the foreboding sign, *Do not play in the fountain. Water chemically doused.*

'That makes me need a fucking piss,' a teenage boy said to the two girls he was with.

At the bottom of the road was the seafront. I walked with my hood up, raindrops bouncing off the plastic protecting my head. I looked at the mucky, disgusting colour the sea had turned and regretted getting out of bed that morning. But I decided to try and make the most out of the situation. It wasn't Clacton's fault that it was so blustery and wet. Maybe if it had been like this when I arrived in Southwold, I wouldn't have been so enthusiastic about it, would have chalked it down as a mistake and vowed never to return. Maybe I wouldn't even have found the plaques with the dedications, or the *Under the Pier* exhibition with the Walking the Dog simulator.

As if to test my resolve, it started to rain even harder. There were some tenacious bastards playing crazy golf. The ball wasn't staying where it was supposed to and a little girl was screaming with unhappiness, tears rolling down her face. I wasn't alone in not having such a lovely time in Clacton. By now it was raining so much I was just looking for anywhere I could escape the pounding. I watched a lady battle with her inside-out umbrella. There was only going to be one winner; there wasn't a single Clacton bin that didn't contain an arrangement of metal spokes that had once been an umbrella. Eventually I found a Wetherspoon's, and opposite it one of those pubs that have an almost identical layout, menu and font as Wetherspoon's.

I ordered a beer. The flyer on my table informed me I was a day too early for Recession Night: £2.50 'til 1am, all shots £1. A man was playing on a fruit machine and was getting so frustrated you wondered why he didn't just not play on the fruit machine. In the beer garden, underneath a huge St George's Flag, sat a couple, shivering, sharing a cigarette. They looked like they hadn't been happy since Henmania.

'Have you seen the sea? It's turned all shit brown!' a man near me explained graphically on his mobile phone.

Pollution on the British coast is a genuine problem. According to the Children's BBC *Newsround* pages (which is where I get most of my news from) 'everything we flush down the toilet ends up in the sea ... in 2003, more than 17,000 cotton buds were washed up on UK beaches.' It's not just cotton buds either. Prescription drugs find their way into the sea, meaning there is a chance that sea life are being subjected to antidepressants.

The Marine Conservation Society is doing its best to help clean up our beaches. They claim that 'Our seas are under immense pressure: too many fish are being taken out, too much rubbish is being thrown in and too little is being done to protect our precious marine wildlife and vital fish stocks.' They provide what is possibly the most alarming statistic of all, that 'There are nearly 2,000 items of rubbish for every kilometre on a beach.'

I went to check into my bed and breakfast. The owner, a cheerful old Essex boy, led me up the stairs to my room and when he left me alone I felt pretty sorry for myself. I was soaking wet from the unbroken rain and exhausted. I found a television set that worked on a *laissez faire* basis: fuzz, fuzz, Sky News, fuzz, fuzz, *Robocop*, fuzz, fuzz, Claudia Winkleman, fuzz. There was a teapot and teacups but no kettle, frayed curtains, a wafer-thin single bed.

That night I tried to get to sleep but the mattress was so uncomfortable and from the next room I could hear every word of a couple's argument. Which would have been fine if it hadn't been such a boring one. Aware that outside my window was a seaside, I went for a midnight wander in Clacton.

I was a little scared as I wandered around. There is a heightened sense of danger at the seaside. A change of clothes hadn't really lifted my spirits, it just meant a new set of clothes to get wet from the still-persistent rain. Worst of all was the sight of the arcades. They were right at Clacton's epicentre, near the clubs and the sea and the high street. You can never escape the brain-frazzling music luring you in to play with the fruit machines and penny pushers and racing simulators. That constant sound nestles in your head, making it impossible to escape. Psychologically, that cannot be a healthy thing – the perennial possibility of success, the klaxons of disappointment.

For the first time since I'd been visiting seasides I started to feel uneasy. Despite only being a couple of counties away I felt so far from home. There was a menace in the air that I left behind, returning to my B&B. I tried again to get to sleep, the jingles of the arcades still in my head, the warning signs I'd seen all day flashing before my eyes: *Dial 999 in emergency and ask for coastguard; do not swim when red flags are present; do not use inflatables; keep off the groynes.*

The following morning, the weather was no better. The rain wasn't going to give in any time soon so I decided to plough on with my journey to Jaywick regardless. The mucky, sad waves were crashing on the shore 10 metres away from where I walked, but not even the wildest wild swimmer would brave dipping a toe in those waters.

According to *The Good Beach Guide*, Clacton-on-Sea is one of the resorts most affected by sewage discharges. What I was seeing was likely to be a result of raw, untreated sewage, which 'gets washed into the sea through combined sewer overflows which discharge storm water, supposedly only in heavy rain'. This is why *The Good Beach Guide* exists: to warn people of the dangers of the sea.

Sadly, the guide started in heartbreaking circumstances; Tony and Daphne Wakefield had tragically lost their six-year-old daughter, Caroline, after she contracted polio while swimming at a contaminated beach. Outraged that raw sewage was being pumped into the sea, the Wakefields published a 'golden list' of clean bathing beaches. This, along with other sea-cleaning campaigns, led to massive investment by the water industry to clean up raw sewage. A rainy Clacton, however, seemed anything other than golden.

I am terrible with directions, which is perhaps why I enjoy the seaside so much. There is always a navigational focal point; three sides of land rather than four makes things much easier. I followed the coast from Clacton to Jaywick, past the deserted children's area and the Toby Carvery, and then walked up the long county road.

Despite the heavy rain I was finally starting to warm to the area. Maybe I had been too quick to be prejudiced towards it. It's wrong to judge a person or a place based on statistics. Whenever possible you should check somewhere yourself. I felt guilty at having prejudged it to such an extent. Then someone driving past wound down their window and shouted 'Wanker!' at me. I fell out of love with Jaywick once more, declaring it to be the worst place I had ever been.

Arriving in Jaywick, Clacton now two miles behind, Deb's Den is on your left: 'Furniture bought and sold', 'House clearances' read the signs; piles and piles of bin bags, rubble and discarded furniture nestled on both sides and at the front. Across the road was a petrol station with a Bargain Booze attached. Jaywick was a town that liked its ceramics; dogs and swans and gnomes festooned most gardens I passed. Then there's Crossways Garage, with a series of battered, out-of-shape cars, waiting for repair after what look like serious accidents. It's a very bold image to greet you on arrival: the aftermath of severe car crashes.

Yet I didn't want to experience the bad side of any seaside. I wanted to find the positives, even in somewhere that had been criticised as much as Jaywick Sands. Even in Essex. I wanted to find out about the personal side of it rather than the economic downturn. I wasn't particularly interested in the financial troubles of the region: it was a notebook I had travelled to the area with rather than a calculator (although I had one on my phone). I wanted to know what it was like for the people who lived there. Who got up day after day, used its shops, drove past the *Welcome to Jaywick* sign, wrote their Jaywick address whenever filling in a form.

Whenever any story such as Jaywick's negative side is exposed, the town will be descended upon by 20-somethings with thick-rimmed black spectacles, haircuts and MacBooks, with the determination to create something 'gritty', using words like 'parallax' and 'social realism'. Admittedly that was exactly what I had done. This was the case with *Jaywick Escapes*, a documentary film produced by Karen Guthrie and Nina Pope, who, like me, were determined to find out more about the seaside town. Guthrie said in an interview with an arthouse website, 'It's weird in Jaywick because everyone talks about the beach being amazing. It's one of the reasons they came there. But if you go there even on a really hot summer's day there's, like, two people and a dog on it.'

The duo had spent weeks at Jaywick before they'd even started recording the documentary. They had been invited there by Essex County Council to do a consultancy; to come up with ideas to get the local community engaged in cultural ideas, specifically around the green space in Jaywick. The duo's experience was that the younger people didn't go out that much. Karen Guthrie said, 'There's actually very little action in Jaywick, incredibly few activities apart from for the old people. Everyone young just stays in and hunkers down on their sofa.'

It wasn't all downbeat, though. As I walked on, I detected a hint of optimism. The names of the roads were noticeably trying to evoke the relaxing and charming, a sense of the countryside and the beach: Jasmine Way, Lavender Walk, Sea Shell Way. They must have been created by a town planner with a sense of romance; or a committee determined to give the place an uplifting image had clearly been giving Jaywick the benefit of the doubt.

By the time I found the beach the sun had started to come out. As the documentary makers suggested would happen, I had it completely to myself. Walking on the sand in your trainers always feels slightly wrong, like drinking water out of a mug.

It was still drizzling as I walked along and a rainbow appeared. A few years ago a video went viral on YouTube called 'The Double Rainbow Guy' – a man who completely breaks down at the beauty of seeing a double rainbow. The video has had 36 million hits and counting. 'It's a double rainbow, all the way. Man that's so intense,' he says, before breaking down completely, sobbing 'It's so beautiful, it's so beautiful,' his mind audibly blown at the sight. But in my head I was even more excited than him when I saw the rainbow in Jaywick. I made him look chilled out. It was a shame no-one was around, a rainbow over the sea is a pretty special sight. I sat down and watched the waves. In the *New York Review of Books* Tim Parks suggests, 'For the rainbow experience to happen we need sunshine, raindrops, and a spectator.' I was the spectator.

It turned out I wasn't alone in finding something worthwhile about Jaywick. Researching the town online you come across Dave's Jaywick website, which is an incredibly positive look at his town that people of any rundown town would be wise to share. Writing about how maligned it has been by authorities and the press, he says, 'In spite of, or maybe because of this a strong feeling of community has evolved in it.'

This is what Jaywick needed. Not articles in broadsheets interviewing Anne, who 'strokes her Alsatian pet dog Fella. "That's why I've got him,"' the *Guardian* article continued. 'Mind you, he was stolen from me as a puppy. The police knew which drug-dealer took him but they wouldn't do anything. I only got him back because someone went round and said "Give him back or your legs'll get broken."'

Earlier, I had walked past a bowling green with a thatched roof, but because I was focusing on the negative I chose to ignore that. When I was in Southwold there must have been numerous negative things I chose to ignore because I was focusing on the positive side of life, the sun was out and I was in a good mood.

In the pub in Clacton, I had concentrated on the man pissed off with the fruit machine. But at the same time there was a couple in the corner, reading a book together. Every time she finished reading she'd look up and wait for a nod, her cue to turn the page. There was a lady with her two sons. She'd taken them there for a Friday after-school meal and it was clearly some kind of ritual. If I had been in a better frame of mind, if I'd read a broadsheet article about how this was the best seaside in the world, it was these people I would have focused on. I wouldn't even have noticed the couple shivering outside with their shared cigarette.

If you are looking for the negative in anything, it's generally easy to find. But the feeling from the people I had come across was, that, despite their potential danger and deprivation in places such as Jaywick, the negative aspects are largely outweighed by the special attractions of living by the seaside. It can be hard to be relaxed somewhere you are so aware of all the warning signs, and are surrounded by the polyphonic orchestra of rejection and defeat from the amusement arcades. But as is the case with the seaside towns I had seen – the benches and plaques in memoriam, the blogs, the articles, the asides you hear when ordering a beer in a pub – the outlook is generally positive. It's hard to judge somewhere harshly when it has its own rainbow.

INTERMISSION

CHAPTER NINE

That's the Way to Do It!

It felt odd to be in London. It's a place I generally spend quite a lot of time in, but I had been in so many seaside towns in recent months that the red double-decker buses, the bustle to get to the escalators on the Underground and the Boris bikes made me feel as much a tourist as those clutching *Shrek the Musical* programmes, happy snapping the Houses of Parliament and the London Eye.

Although I was temporarily away from seaside towns, I was in London on seaside business. Covent Garden was playing host to one of the seaside's most iconic couples: Punch and Judy. It was Mr Punch's 350th birthday, and a convention was being held in his honour. This was being held at the Strand Palace Hotel, an appropriately named venue: Strand is named after the German word for beach, so-called because the shores of the Thames once reached up to what is now known as The Strand.

I hate Punch and Judy. Hate is a strong word; and I hate Punch and Judy. I'm a bit scared of puppets. I don't trust people who aren't. Which is why sitting in the hotel restaurant with a Mr Punch either side of me was not my ideal way to spend an evening. Earlier in the afternoon I had walked around Covent Garden taking in the eccentricities of the birthday celebrations, which included fancy-dress parades with trombone-fronted brass bands and hundreds of Mr Punches being waved in the air while singing 'Happy Birthday'. I have never seen so many spangly waistcoats and Union Flag top hats.

The fact the convention was for Mr Punch's birthday rather than his anniversary goes a long way to identify the esteem with which he is regarded (even if not by me). To many, Punch and Judy are cherished, a way of life: he entertains and pays the mortgages of all the Punch Professors, as they like to call themselves, who were surrounding me at the convention. I felt like an impostor with so many people treating a puppet with such affection, as if he was a revered elder statesman, a beloved national treasure. Mr Punch was being talked about like he was Sir David Frost.

An early Mr Punch fan was the diarist Samuel Pepys, who saw him as part of a puppet show in Covent Garden (hence the setting for the birthday celebrations). On 9 May 1662, Pepys noted in a diary entry that he enjoyed 'an Italian puppet play that is within the rayles there, which is very pretty, the best that ever I saw...' In 1962, at Mr Punch's 300th birthday celebrations, a commemorative inscription was unveiled: *Near this spot Punch's Puppet Show was first performed in England and witnessed by Samuel Pepys.*

Glyn Edwards, the master puppeteer who had organised the birthday celebrations, which he called *The Big Grin*, spoke as part of the extensive publicity in the lead-up to the event, talking about the evolution of the audiences and their relationship with Mr Punch. 'He's had to keep in tune with the social climate. When Judy refers to the baby as little Asbo it gets a laugh,' he said about the latest addition to the Punch family. 'New characters you are likely to see as part of the ensemble today now include Mr Bonus the Banker and a health and safety officer, complete with a clipboard and high-vis jacket – who ends up in Mr Punch's sausage machine.'

If there was one thing that united the people I was sharing a table with, all of us looking forward to tucking into the carvery that was being provided, it was being the type of person to tut at the mention of a health and safety officer, people who Biro-circle *Grumpy Old Men* in the *Radio Times*.

Punch and Judy have regularly faced criticism that they are too violent for children. In 2004 a council in Cornwall banned a show following complaints that it promoted domestic violence. Having read about the origins of Mr Punch in the build-up to the celebrations and being surrounded by so many people who were obsessed with him, I felt guilty that I'd never actually seen a show.

My mum and dad never took me to see Punch and Judy and it was one of many things I am eternally thankful for. Beyond the fact there was a dog and a crocodile, my knowledge was limited.

The man I was sitting next to had introduced himself as a Punch Professor and had been involved in the celebrations that afternoon. I thought now was the time to learn; maybe I had been missing out on something? I asked if he could explain the storyline to me, provide me with his own director's commentary. He didn't quite seem to believe I could have got through my whole live never having seen a show. It felt as if I'd told him I'd never seen an episode of *Friends*, never eaten a Wispa. He patiently explained the basic plot of Punch and Judy.

The show starts with the arrival of Mr Punch, quickly followed on stage by Judy. They kiss and Judy asks Punch to look after the baby. The rest of the plot centres around his failure in doing so, before Mr Punch ends up killing some or all of the cast. I was slightly puzzled by the explanation but my Punch Professor nodded his head sagely and I didn't want him to start questioning what it was all about: 'Oh my God, it's all meaningless!' The story, I sensed, was all in the performance and the characters. It must have had something about it to have endured the centuries in seaside booths across the UK; generations of children being treated to their first-ever Punch and Judy shows complete with rolling pins, strings of sausages and boos for the baddies.

The man on the other side of me at the dining table told me he worked as a clown. Next to him his friend explained that he had worked as a Punch Professor for 50 years and loved it.

'The job hasn't changed at all,' he told me. 'The children in 1962 were just as sweet and lovely and excitable as they are today.' The clown's wife returned with a tray of drinks.

'They didn't have any real ale on tap,' she said, apologetically, but I hope this is okay.' She presented her husband with a bottle of Old Speckled Hen and a half-pint glass.

'Well done,' he said. 'Old Speckled Hen is quite nice.'
I was surprised how normal everyone was. At first they were talking shop, chatting about the day's events and using phrases like 'We've done very well with the weather.' When the formalities were dispensed with it was mainly nice people talking about everyday things. Two Punch Professors in full costume talked about *The Apprentice*. Lord Sugar had been firing the wrong candidates, they agreed. A man told everyone about his recent deep vein thrombosis attacks, another how he had suffered with a burst appendix while working as an entertainer on a cruise ship. This didn't make for ideal dinner conversation, but then the table filled with people of a certain age, and increasingly that is something all of us have in common, whether we're puppeteers, clowns or bank managers.

I tried to carry on my conversation with the clown about the seaside, but he apologised, saying he couldn't really hear me because he was a little deaf. The Punch Professor next to me had also explained that he was partially deaf, painting the image of generations of children screaming in their ears.

At the head of the table was what I was hoping to find: the young enthusiast of a dying art form. Whether it's crown green bowling or beekeeping, metal detecting, country dancing or stamp collecting, you know there is going to be a ten-year-old child with enthusiasm inherited from a parent or grandparent, and that they are likely to be slightly ashamed of it in years to come. There he was on my table, destined to explode onto the Punch and Judy scene like Michael Owen at the 1998 World Cup. Increasingly, people who are involved with this kind of hobby have the expectations of previous generations breathing down on them, but are competing with more accessible and commonplace methods of entertainment. Like any industry, Punch and Judy can only flourish if there are lads like this to carry on the tradition.

A love for something like Punch and Judy is likely to be instilled in you at a very early age. I like football and support Liverpool, and that is entirely due to the fact that in 1988, on the day of the Liverpool versus Wimbledon FA Cup Final (the final result of which is unimportant), an aunt sent me a Liverpool scarf and pendant that I hung on my bunk bed. From that moment on, posters of Liverpool players covered my bedroom walls and my pencil cases always had Liverpool FC scrawled on them in Biro or scratched on with a pair of compasses.

Maybe if instead of that pendant I had been given a Punch and Judy kit, I would have fallen in love with those characters, I would have known the script and the story inside out and have been putting on glove puppet shows to my friends at school. This annual Punch and

Judy convention would be the highlight of my year. For the most part people aren't strange, they're not oddballs. We're often just influenced by things that are beyond our control.

There have been a succession of famous Punch Professors over the years. One fondly remembered Punch Professor was a man called Frank Edmonds. His father Harry had been a Punch Professor in the 19th century. The story is told how Harry was so good at Mr Punch that his booth was set alight by envious Pierrots. Frank used exactly the same script as his father used for all those years, and it was believed that Harry had learned that same script in turn, which could possibly have dated back as early as 1871.

In 1916 Frank Edmonds ran away from school in order to become a Punch and Judy man, and he would walk 'as far as 20 miles a day, pushing his booth on a handcart and sleeping beneath it at night'. His life seemed very straightforward. In the summer he worked on the beach, in winter at Christmas parties. When he married this wandering life ended and he took a pitch on Weymouth Beach, one of the original seaside resorts.

Edmonds was particularly constrained in being a puppeteer because he was left handed, which was very rare in the trade. He had to make himself improve his co-ordination, resulting in this very sweet quote from an interview he did with the *Southern Times*: 'Now I can do anything with either hand equally well and can hold my hands above my head for hours without getting tired.' Most notable about Edmonds was that he used a live dog, Toby, in his act, until it ran away during the War. As a mark of respect, Toby was never replaced, not even by a puppet. Edmonds ended up working as a Mr Punch his whole life, a career spanning more than 50 years.

Another Mr Punch before the war was John Rodber who, like Edmonds, is written about in the book *That's The Way to Do It*, profiling Punch Professors of the ages. Rodber worked for Westminster Bank and performed puppet shows in his spare time. The bank did not allow employees to make money elsewhere, so all his shows were for charity. But the more he performed the puppet shows, the more he started to dislike his job at the bank, so his wife Joy urged him to leave: 'His employers were incredulous … and wanted to send him to a psychiatrist.' Soon life in a bank was a thing of the past. The two of them opened an art shop in Bridport and from 1950 started doing Punch and Judy shows when the shop was closed, eventually ending up performing the show on television to huge audiences, being transported in limousines.

One other notable Punch Professor, although this time fictional, was Tony Hancock, who was himself from the seaside, having grown up in Bournemouth. Hancock co-wrote the script to the film *The Punch and Judy Man* with Philip Oakes, and the movie was shot in Bognor Regis, chosen for its sandy beaches.

Although I found puppets annoying rather than scary, Hancock was terrified. Pupaphobia can cause panic attacks, dizziness, anxiety, a sense of doom and nausea. During filming, the Punch Professor Joe Hastings operated the puppets in any scene where Hancock didn't need to be seen operating them due to the troubled star's fear of the wooden objects. When Hastings died shortly after the completion of the film, Hancock sent him 'a large floral arrangement in the form of the puppet'.

The film, about a struggling beach entertainer who dreams of a better life, wasn't a success. The *Daily Express* was particularly unimpressed: 'I won't bother you with the story,' they wrote, 'which on paper will look even flimsier than the film.' Philip Oakes found the film 'sad viewing, flashes of genuine brilliance intermingled with moments of truth in acting, but ultimately overshadowed by the promise of what might have been.' Despite this, Hancock had an affection for the film 'that stayed with him to the end of his days'.

Back at the Punch and Judy 350th birthday celebrations, with all of us full of roast potatoes, Yorkshire pudding and little stuffing balls, it was time for the entertainment. On stage was Mel Meller, a magician. 'I would like to say hello to this lovely lady in the audience, what's your name?… No, no … the *lovely* lady.'

As with so many people I had met that day, there was something of a bygone world about Mel Meller. You could tell he'd made a few ladies of a certain age swoon on cruise ships on every ocean. He had an effortless charm, an ease with the people he was talking to.

What was happening that weekend wasn't so much about the audiences these puppeteers, clowns and magicians had been entertaining in Covent Garden. It was about the gathering together of like-minded people. All year long the Punch and Judy guys were spread out across the country, hiding under brightly striped canvases in Southend, Margate, Ilfracombe, Skegness, because there were children who needed entertaining.

Browsing a Punch and Judy forum online, I found a gentle and charming reminder of this, posted by someone with the username Miraiker: *'I thought I'd just remind everybody, while they worry about the weather, the slopes and all manner of other things just how lucky we all are to have Punch in our lives. What a variety of strange and lovely people we come across over the course of the season. The audiences – variable I admit but we get to perform our shows to mostly appreciative families who come and chat afterwards, buy us cups of coffee and occasionally cake. Just think of all the poor people who do proper jobs. Isn't Punch great?'*

Even anyone with the most severe case of pupaphobia would have been hard pressed to respond with a 'No' to this. People who come to these events and contribute to these forums have chosen puppetry as a form of escapism. It's a conscious decision to live close to the lapping waves of Clacton, Weymouth and Weston-super-Mare, rather than Kettering, Slough or Doncaster. This is why they seemed more normal than I had expected them to be. In their day-to-day lives they are the eccentrics. They are the odd character, they're 'the Punch and Judy guy'. It's an odd way to earn your living. I can imagine that as a consequence their friends and family treat them in a slightly unusual way, most not conscious of the fact they are even doing it.

Sometimes when someone has a certain occupation or pastime others can feel unable to bring the subject around to anything else. Eric Morecambe's son, Gary Bartholomew, wrote a book about his dad, *Funny Man*, in which he explained his father's difficulties at social gatherings. 'My line of business is so different from the norm,' Eric said, 'that I have found it difficult to communicate convincingly with local people at parties and suchlike, and no doubt they have found the same problem with me. It sounds boring and conceited to say it, but I am too much of an attraction to be accepted with ease.'

That is true of many people doing unusual jobs: television personalities, puppeteers, assassins. It's much more complicated than being a teacher, a shopkeeper, an optician. At times they must find it difficult to mingle in normal social situations. They must have to answer the same questions over and over again. But when they are amongst their own there is a mutual understanding. This is what I was witnessing in the dining room full of people celebrating Mr Punch's 350th birthday.

They were relaxed; they knew there was no pressure to perform, show off or explain what they were doing. They didn't have to talk about being a puppeteer, because they were all puppeteers. They were all people doing a job they loved, who had spent their lives at the seaside, pretending their hands were crocodiles, making children cheer and giggle and boo and clap. This was their form of escape. While everyone else was getting away from real life by heading to the seaside, the Mr Punches were leaving the coast, coming to the heart of the bustle of central London, to get away from it all.

Part Three

SOUTH

CHAPTER TEN

A Beano to Margate

There is no stronger image of a day out at the British seaside than in the episode of *Only Fools and Horses* when Del Boy organises the annual Nag's Head coach trip to the seaside – 'a beano to Margate' as Boycie described it, stopping off at the halfway house on the way. The episode left no seaside cliché unturned: ring doughnuts, sunshine, 'Kiss me quick' hats, funfairs, Del in his best suit drinking piña coladas.

Perhaps as traditional as all of these activities was the moment of honest truth between Del and Rodney. There is something about the seaside that makes people open up. You feel closer to people because you are away from home. At every seaside you'll see people experiencing Del Boy-style outpourings of love and tenderness; perhaps it's because you are on the edge of the country, with wide-open spaces everywhere; perhaps this is why there are so many marriage proposals at the seaside, why it has played such a part in the lives of millions.

In the *Only Fools and Horses* episode, Rodney and his wife Cassandra had been married for a year and Rodney admitted to his brother that he was starting to have doubts about it. Del put his arm round him, told him he had done well and that their mum would be proud. 'Cassandra's an achiever,' he said to Rodney. 'Just like me. I'm an achiever. I've never actually achieved anything, though.'

This is why people go to the seaside: to reminisce, to become closer to people, those you see on a regular basis, drink with, live with and work with. That is the origin of the word 'beano' – in the 18th-century landowners would treat the farm workers and their families to a 'bean feast' or a night of drinking and dancing. This was later adopted by the mill owners, who'd take the whole workforce away *en masse*. That evolved into the coach trip, as seen in *Only Fools and Horses*. It wasn't called a jolly boys' outing until writer John Sullivan put the words into David Jason's script and the term has been used ever since. That outing from Peckham to Margate was the equivalent of paintballing today: bonding, fun, a chance to get dressed up, do things you wouldn't ordinarily do in your day-to-day life. Margate is also the destination in Graham Swift's *Last Orders*, a journey to scatter a war veteran's ashes.

Practically every person I had spoken to about the British seaside had mentioned Margate, sometimes disparagingly, sometimes affectionately, almost always with a sense of sadness. Nowhere, it seemed, captured the seaside more than Margate with its heyday and decline. I decided to make Margate the start of the southern leg of my seaside tour – a journey that would take me from the Kent coastline all the way down to Cornwall.

I went down to Margate on the train from St Pancras, leaving the capital behind me. By the time I arrived I was practically the only person remaining on what had been a bustling carriage, but that emptied as we stopped at Ashford International and Canterbury. Clearly people were not in the mood for going to the seaside on this particular day. Not a jolly boys' outing in sight.

Within minutes of getting off the train, the sea to my left, I glimpsed a building that looked as if detonation was imminent. In bold capital letters was the name DREAMLAND. It may as well have spelled out 'Pathos'. This is what I had gone to Margate to see. I didn't realise it would be quite so easy to find. Walking to the top of an adjacent car park, you can get a view of what is being protected by the barbed wire and tall fences: an abandoned rollercoaster. Beyond the graffitied walls, padlocks, security signs and wasteland, you could make out the sea. Walking near the wire fencing and the abandoned corrugated iron, it's impossible to think of anything other than tetanus jabs. On what used to be a door someone had written *'Happy Birthday Arsehole. Fagz. '97.'* Fagz is probably a balding deputy headmaster now, or working in insurance, grateful for the anonymity of his late 90s nickname.

Despite the twisty ghostly 'lostness' of Margate, it was clear that there had once been enjoyment here. *Pie Days and Holidays*, a project on the seafront devised by Katie Kneale, comprised a mural, paintings and memories from locals, collecting and recording holiday stories from Margate people. Claire wrote, 'We've been thinking about moving here for about two years – the architecture is so proud, it's got glamour, it's not faded, it just needs a polish.' Another, slightly more mysterious vignette recalled that 'Along the seafront there used to be a man from Sunbeam Photography. He used to chat up the ladies and always liked my mum. His monkey was tiny and agile and used to jump on and off our shoulders while he was chatting to mum.'

There is honesty too. 'We had everything,' Helen remembered. 'Dreamland. Sun Deck. On the end of the pier they used to have a little theatre with Pierrot shows. At Dreamland there was a zoo with tigers, monkeys, bears. I knew it was going downhill when I came here one day in 1976 and there was just no-one around.'

It was a man called John Henry Iles who bought the property that became Dreamland. Iles wanted to turn what had previously been a music and dance hall into an American-style theme park. His plan worked; for decades Margate was as popular as any other seaside town. It had everything: close to London, good beach, accessible. Dreamland's main attraction was the wooden rollercoaster ride, which opened in 1921; in its first three months an extra half a million visitors arrived in Margate. The rollercoaster is visible from vantage points all across town, and when it was running the screams would be audible to anyone walking down the high street.

The problem was that when the rollercoaster became old and disused, it was still just as visible. Anyone walking through Margate can see what used to be enjoyable and fun. 'I'd have gone on that,' they think as they pass its ruins, no screams of enjoyment audible as you walk past the closed-down shops. Just an occasional sigh.

Dreamland had been particularly vibrant in the 1920s. Later on, the ballroom hosted gigs by bands such as The Who and The Rolling Stones. But after 80 years of operation it was announced that Dreamland would close to be turned into housing and retail units. This prompted the formation of the Save Dreamland Campaign in 2003. There seemed to be as many campaigns as there were seaside resorts.

The Dreamland Trust was intent on saving Margate's amusement park. The rollercoaster is now Grade II* listed, as is the cinema building. This involved contributions from the Heritage Lottery Fund, the Government's Sea Change programme and the district council. The plan was for Dreamland not to be a dry historical exhibit, 'but a living, breathing, multi-sensory environment telling Dreamland's rich historic story'. Part of the Dreamland project was to teach about the importance of Margate historically in primary schools. It is a shame for those growing up in the area that it will likely be just another history lesson of something from a bygone age. But who knows? Maybe by the time they are in a position to leave home they will choose to stay in Margate, proud to be living in such a vibrant and important seaside town.

With the wooden rollercoaster hanging over me, I walked down the high street. It was the by now familiar combination of closed-down outlets, arcades, charity shops and places to sell gold. One glimpse of promise was Popportunity – what was once a shop had been converted into an indoor market where people sold jewellery, homemade cards and food. Visitors to Margate ten years previously would have just seen the sense of abandonment, but now at least there was a sense that people were making it better.

The plans were that over the next two years Dreamland would be a place for locals and tourists to enjoy again; under the Thanet skies there would be screams of enjoyment once more rather than just audible sighs of frustration.

It wasn't just the Dreamland project that was gave Margate cause for optimism: there was also its much-hyped Turner Contemporary gallery. Tracey Emin, the artist most associated with Margate today, was hugely in support of the gallery: 'The brilliant thing about Turner Contemporary is that it has given people hope that things are going to change here and also put Margate back on the map.'

Emin is a staunch supporter of Margate, as people should be of their home towns, and in the build-up to her exhibition, *She Lay Down Beneath the Sea,* she wrote an open letter to local residents asking them to come. 'I wanted to do something special,' she said, about her exhibition at the Turner gallery, 'because it is Margate.' Reviewing the exhibition, the *Sunday Times* said that, 'it's a beautiful effect, and the proximity of the lapping water seems to have inspired a set of gentle reflections in Emin, on love and blokes and paddling.' Sadly, the exhibition was no longer running by the time of my visit, but I was keen to see what else the gallery had on offer.

It was midday by now, as I walked across Margate seafront, hands thrust deeply in pockets. 'Don't mind us,' the waves seemed to be calling out, reading the morning's newspapers. It didn't take me long to see the gallery: it stood out on the seafront, a tall glass building very clearly belonging to a different area to that of Dreamland.

Turner Contemporary opened in Margate in 2011, a dynamic visual arts organisation that believes in making art open, relevant and fulfilling for all. This seemed an exciting prospect; entry was free, perfect for an area that really needed rejuvenating in some way. It turned out that it's not just Emin who was associated with Margate. The seaside town was also important for another artist, JMW Turner, who remarked to the influential writer and art critic John Ruskin that '… the skies over Thanet are the loveliest in all Europe'.

Turner was sent to Margate aged 11, having been sent by his parents to school there. He returned to sketch here aged 21 and became a regular visitor. He stayed at a seafront guesthouse with a landlady called Mrs Booth, whom 'he loved as much as the sea and the skies', and it is on that same site that the Turner gallery has been built. In all, more than

100 of Turner's works were inspired by the East Kent coast and his association with the area was strong enough for the gallery to take his name.

In the gallery café a man drank a glass of red wine, reading Tim Dowling's column in the *Guardian*. A man with one of those fashionable beards looked very pleased with himself as he carefully pondered what to order from the menu. Others sat, tapping at their computers or swiping their phones. Margate's regeneration could have been financed entirely by everyone in the Turner Contemporary café bar selling their MacBooks.

I went upstairs and from the big glass windows the sea forms part of the exhibition. Several of us watched an Audi struggling to reverse from its bay in the car park. Beyond that were the waves, and we all watched, hypnotically absorbing the rhythms. For all the artwork on display in the gallery, Alex Katz canvases covering entire walls, prime-coloured pop art which the gallery's visitors were cross-referencing with their visitors' handbook, I looked out at the sea for longer than at any painting.

The credit for this revolution in seaside art is generally given to a government initiative called *Sea Change*, whose mission was 'to use culture to make a difference to seaside resorts, contributing to sustainable, social and economic regeneration'. The journalist and agricultural writer Steve Rose tells how 'between 2008 and 2010, *Sea Change* directed £37m towards 34 cultural improvement projects around the coastline', including Bexhill, Margate, and controversially, Hastings.

It was Margate's fellow Kent resort of Hastings that my travels took me to next. Almost the first thing I became aware of as I walked through the Old Town were the stickers and posters on shop windows and pub noticeboards and in the windows of homes persuading us to 'Say no to Jerwood at the Stade!' The controversy about the multi-million-pound Jerwood gallery that had recently opened peaked on Bonfire Night, where instead of the traditional guy or an effigy of a Tory politician, it was a mock-up of the Jerwood Gallery being burned.

It's not that the people of Hastings are less interested in art than the residents of Margate. It was entirely about the location – the centuries of tradition did not want to be tarnished with something so clearly 21st century. Working fishermen did not want to be stopped by visitors to the area to ask if they knew the wi-fi password. The Stade is the shingle beach in Hastings Old Town, the main feature of which is the collection of tall black fishing huts, known as net shops. The height of the huts is due to the lack of space; they had to build them upwards rather than across to conserve space. This is where the spirit of Hastings is: the Old Town, the brasseries, cafés and a little bookshop which turns into a bring-your-own-booze Thai restaurant in the evenings.

It was the fishermen who owned these huts who sparked the controversy in the seaside town: one survey suggested that 82 per cent of them were against the gallery opening there. The fishermen play a big role in Hastings. There are places to buy fresh fish everywhere and I went to one of the many fish-and-chips restaurants for lunch. Alisha served behind the counter. I know she's called Alisha because a man in white overalls came in through the Staff Only door saying, 'Alisha, you left the back door unlocked, you twat!' I sat down at the table and waited for our food. She told a customer she had stopped smoking 31 days ago.

'Good!' the lady ordering chips and pickled eggs said to her. 'You need to look after your skin.' She talked about her 41-year-old twin boys. 'We love the chips here', she said to Alisha. 'We've always come here. I tell all of my friends to come here. Good food is important. I've never tasted a McDonald's.'

The seaside is a place where you can have unusual food. Going on holiday used to be so exciting. Italy for its pizzas, France for its croissants, wine and cheeses, but it's a long time since paella has been exotic. At the seaside, there is this chance for you to be out of your comfort zone with jellied eels, winkles, whelks. Admittedly I was only having fish and chips, but this time it was special because I was eating them from a plate. I was even using cutlery. It's important to feel that you're experiencing something you can't get elsewhere; eating strange-tasting and -smelling food. That used to be one of the treats of going on holiday. There was nothing more exciting than someone coming back from school holidays with a big bag of 'Liam's been to Florida' foreign sweets.

I walked on past a pub that offered grilled sardines, smoked salmon, calamari rings, prawn cocktail, homemade fish pie, grilled halibut with chilli and garlic in a mussel and herb broth. That day in Hastings I just couldn't stop eating, it was so hard to resist the little vans and shops selling pots of pickled fresh things. I ordered some jellied eels and picked at them with a cocktail stick with no idea what I was supposed to be doing. It's good for food to be confusing sometimes.

I continued along the whole length of the seafront, then ambled back to the Stade once more. Despite the local protests it was clear that the Jerwood Gallery was there to stay. It didn't seem to aesthetically harm its environment. The protests prove the strong community spirit in Hastings. That was already clear from the reaction to the pier burning down in 2010 and the resulting determined campaign to have it restored. Not a single conversation I'd had with people relating to Hastings had been anything other than the highest praise. Even people who didn't live there responded with wide eyes when I told them I'd just been to Hastings. They'd been there for a day, had a friend who lived there, had spent time there growing up. 'Oh, Hastings!' they'd say, and for a moment they were there again, on the beach or in the Old Town.

I had friends who lived in Hastings, so a spare room was provided, meaning I could stay up late drinking and talking about the seaside. Perhaps biased because of this, Hastings was possibly my favourite of all the seaside places I had been to. I really got the sense from those I spoke to that people who live in Hastings do so because they love it rather than because it's somewhere they've ended up through work, relationships or whatever. It epitomised what the seaside should be. 'One day I'm going to move to Hastings,' I thought to myself, walking around the Old Town, but I'd said the same about practically every seaside I had been to.

'Please don't tell anyone how cool it is here,' a girl said to me in the pub that night. 'We don't want anyone finding out about it. Brighton used to be like this, then everyone turned up and ruined it all. Let's keep this our little secret.' I knew exactly what she meant, and promised her I wouldn't tell a soul.

CHAPTER ELEVEN

The Beachy Head Chaplaincy Team

It was my friend Tamsin who told me about the Beachy Head Chaplaincy Team. As with so many of my conversations, this prompted exchanges of seaside memories. I told her about the week I'd spent working in Scarborough, the pier at Southwold, the community spirit of Hastings. She mentioned that there was a pub at Beachy Head where the bar staff had to be trained in counselling.

Everyone I spoke to was dropping clues, hinting at the stories of the British seaside I was so desperate to uncover. I knew that Beachy Head was a suicide hotspot, but had never been there, or to neighbouring Eastbourne. I discovered there was a group of people dedicated to approaching suicidal people and talking to them, making sure they are okay. I wanted to find out more about their work, and arranged to meet the Beachy Head Chaplaincy Team to discuss their work.

On the train to Eastbourne, I listened to an episode of a radio show called *This American Life* on Chicago Public Radio. It was about a suicide hotspot on a bridge in China where a man had single-handedly given himself the role of talking people out of jumping from the bridge. He estimated that he had saved 174 lives, counselled 5,150 people. His method, as observed by a US journalist, was to approach the potential victim and say, 'I want to take your picture.' Once he had done that he'd say, 'And now I want to punch you in the face. How dare you do this? You are somebody's son. I am going to punch you now. Nothing is worth this. There is no problem we cannot solve.'

I couldn't quite imagine the Beachy Head Chaplaincy Team being the sort of people to threaten punching someone in the face. As the train pulled into Eastbourne, I was intrigued to know how the English seaside did deal with people in a similar state of distress.

All seaside towns have benches dedicated to people's memories, but nowhere can this be more notable than in Eastbourne. What struck me was how well maintained they were, with fresh flowers and wreaths. Also prominent were the residential homes; a care worker holding the door open for a couple struggling with walking sticks and shopping bags. Eastbourne is a popular destination for those retiring to the seaside. It's easy to understand why, too: the views are beautiful and there is no bustle, no chaos. Just a pretty seaside town.

I wasn't meeting the Beachy Head team until later in the day so I had time to look around, observe what was happening. I wasn't exactly sure where I was going, but I knew I couldn't ask for directions. If I asked anyone how to get to Beachy Head I was worried they would rugby tackle me to the ground, tell me how much I had to live for. Instead I just walked in the direction of the white chalk cliffs I could see far in the distance. I was in a good mood, the way people often are when travelling. I would be lying if I said I hadn't enjoyed choosing a playlist of songs to listen to on my MP3 player while walking along the windswept, bleak coastal path.

I was pretty happy. The walk was similar to those treks I had made so many times in Scarborough, just walking and enjoying the constant motion of the waves and the comforting familiarity of sand and fresh air. There weren't many of us on the beach. A couple walked a dog. A pretty girl in a parka gazed at the horizon, hands buried deep in her pockets. I walked and walked; the sea was turquoise and choppy, bouncing like a mosh pit. It was good to see a body of water that had some energy in it, that was really making an effort to splash for the tourists. Morrissey segued into The Cure on my headphones as I looked up at the enormous cliffs. It was then that the significance of Beachy Head hit me. The cliff may as well have toppled 90 degrees, flattening me into the sand. It had taken me this long to comprehend the fact that was staring me in the face. The reason Beachy

Head has a reputation as a suicide hotspot is because this is where people come when they feel at their worst. I took off my headphones.

Next to me, looking up, was a thin man with spectacles who was wearing what can only be described as a party shirt; a Hawaiian, blue flowery number. He looked so sad. This man clearly had things on his mind. I looked around and the pretty girl in the parka was also walking in our direction, stopping occasionally, allowing the waves to crash onto her boots. There we were, the three of us, all on our own, all of us thinking about stuff. Going to Beachy Head and not thinking about suicide is like going to Disneyland and not thinking about Mickey Mouse.

I still had a couple of hours before my meeting with the Chaplaincy Team and so climbed to the top of the cliff. I say 'climbed', I mean 'walked along the designated path'. I am not much of an adventurer. The view at the top was worth my asthmatic wheezing. Just off the coast was a red and white striped lighthouse. In 2011, Trinity House announced that it would no longer be responsible for painting and restoring the red and white stripes, so people visiting in years to come will just see an increasingly faded landmark. I thought of people coming here whom the Chaplains would have to talk to, and it was sadder than I ever thought possible, that people get to the point where they think This Is It.

Further along the cliff a hang-gliding lesson was beginning. Ten or so people were in the air, reaching 20 feet above the cliff. Their view must have been spectacular. The beauty next to the overhanging pathos was almost too much for me. I videoed it on my phone, thinking 'This is like a metaphor,' but I couldn't think for what. It was far too cold for that kind of thing.

At the coastguard hut the Operations Manager, Ben, who had been outside cleaning one of the Chaplaincy patrol cars when I arrived, offered me a cup of tea. He had been involved with the Chaplaincy since late 2007.

'It's all about the protection of lives,' Ross Hardy told me from the other settee. This room must have been an incredibly welcome place in recent times; volunteers returning after patrolling, responding to calls, battling with the sea winds, desperate to be able to get back to the settee as the kettle boiled. 'I really needed this,' they'd say, dunking a biscuit.

Ross was the Chaplaincy's founder. He told me they weren't just dealing with people locally, but those who come from across the country and from around the world with the intention of ending their lives at Beachy Head. They're also dealing with people who may have depression or mental illness; they may not be suicidal but have been drawn to this spot.

'It's one of those places that's quite desolate,' Ross told me. 'Certain people feel very at home with that environment. Primarily we deal with saving lives, but also it's talking to people in their hour of need. The team work 24 hours a day, seven days a week. We also respond to the police and to missing person searches for the coastguard at Dover. We deal with people we may come across when patrolling, or we may be called to search for them specifically because we've been given information that they are heading to Beachy Head. We get reports from members of the public or pub staff, or anyone from bus drivers to shopkeepers.'

I was slightly nervous to be in the company of Ross and Ben. I love meeting people who do interesting jobs, but I worried that I may have been a little out of my depth with this. When they introduced themselves, they alerted me to the fact that they rarely agreed to do interviews and were wary about what was written about them. They are very careful about what information is made available on their website. I wanted to respect their wishes while at the same time finding out about what it was they did.

I asked how they identify suicidal people. 'It's all about having strong listening skills,' Ross replied. 'When we approach someone we first explain who we are and that we're from the Chaplaincy Team. We tell them what we do, why we are there and we get to the bottom of what has brought them to Beachy Head. It is important they know we are experienced at dealing with suicidal people. For them to acknowledge they are suicidal makes a big difference. But often they aren't suicidal. They're just unhappy, worried, potentially they are going to harm themselves, for whatever reason they have been drawn here.'

The Beachy Head Chaplaincy Team deal with many people whose biggest problem is that they have never had anyone to talk to about how they were feeling.

'For us to say "You are safe with us" is the most crucial part of the process,' Ross continued. 'Next we engage what we call Active Listening, in which we encourage them to share the deepest issue of what's going on, what has brought them to these feelings of being suicidal. It might not be just one reason, but a series of incidents, an accumulation of problems. We talk to them. Make sure they're okay. We are there to encourage life over death. Our team are highly trained in suicide prevention. To date we have saved the lives of something in the region of 1,500 people. Unfortunately it's something we get a lot of practice at, though.'

Not for the first time that day I was lost for words. I thought of all the benches in memoriam, the tiny wooden crosses planted in dedication at the top of the cliffs. 'Do the volunteers get affected by what they have to witness?' I asked, directing the question at Ben, a volunteer. He's a church minister in the town, and runs the Salvation Army. His main responsibilities are the rotas for the shifts. Ben looks after their welfare, cares for them pastorally as well as patrolling and doing frontline work.

'We're very blessed in that very few of our volunteers actually see anyone jump off,' Ben told me. He was slightly older than Ross, perhaps late forties, and like Ross was wearing the red polo shirt with the Chaplaincy logo. 'The majority have been well protected from that. Myself and Ross have seen a fair few and there are others on the team who are catching us up now. But on the whole it doesn't happen that regularly in front of one of our teams. In the event it does happen I will attend, check they're okay, stay in the back of the car for the rest of the shift just in case they needed someone.'

Ross explained about Critical Incident Debrief, where they talk to volunteers on the scene, then a couple of days later they'll talk to them again, and then once more perhaps a week later, to assess how they are getting on. The main thing was to actually talk about the situation because that releases the pressure. There was a team counsellor they could refer team members to if necessary: situations can be quite harrowing even if the incident ends with a safe return. Team welfare has to come first.

'Is there a positive side to that?' I asked. 'There must be a huge feeling of satisfaction when you succeed in getting someone talking and to reconsider their position.'

'It is incredibly rewarding when someone comes back from the edge,' Ross continued. 'It's someone's life and a team member has been there at someone's darkest hour. They have actually been able to help someone, persuade them to come back from the edge, make the choice for life. It is an amazing experience to go through, the process of what has brought them there and managing to resolve it, which is why the team put up with the more harrowing moments. But even in those situations you are dealing with someone in such deep despair that it can take its toll. There's the balance to make sure that in an exciting rescue the team don't feel overburdened with the crisis they are facing.'

And they do hear back from people. That's the one thing I had really wanted to know about working with such extreme situations. It's not always the case. Sometimes people feel the need to move on. But equally some people keep in contact. In fact, the team had heard back from someone that afternoon. Sometimes they make a point of coming back to meet the team a few years later, sit down on the settee, have a cup of tea, maybe not with the person who saved them but certainly someone wearing the same uniform, the same logo on their shirt. They are in a better place and feel strong enough to make the journey back to the little hut and engage about their experience of what happened.

'They are the encouraging moments,' Ross told me. 'Their life was saved that day and you know they have subsequently improved. It's good for us. Good for our volunteers.'

It is not just the Beachy Head Chaplaincy Team that is so reliant on its volunteers. All across the beaches of the UK there are volunteers doing vital work. One such organisation is the Royal National Lifeboat Institution, who have saved around 140,000 lives at seas since 1824. At most seaside resorts you will see a lifeboat museum, or a gift shop, charity shop, or even just a lifeboat-shaped collection box in the local newsagents. On their website the RNLI explain that they provide, on call, a 24-hour lifeboat search and rescue service and a seasonal lifeguard service'. On average, lifeboat crews launch 24 times a day nationally; without volunteers they wouldn't be able to save lives at sea.

In 2011, on average 22 people were rescued every day by lifeboat crew members. Although there are pages of statistics available about the number of lives they have saved and people they have helped, it is impossible to calculate how many people they have helped just by raising awareness in schools and youth clubs and by their visibility at the beach. Our seafronts are blessed with people devoting their lives to others.

The volunteers with the Beachy Head Chaplaincy team are from churches in the local areas and from a range of backgrounds: they included an ex-Chief Superintendent of the Metropolitan Police, a builder, church ministers, people who work in the NHS, a doctor, a landscape gardener, and the unemployed. There are people in their 20s and those in their 70s. Each person has their specific skills. They work in teams of two, and there is always a response team who will back them up. In the team of two they have their specific roles in the intervention. It is a long way from when Ross and his team first started, just a few of them working during the evenings. Ross worked six nights a week, and as time went on was joined by others. The level of the operation in Beachy Head is unique.

Ross told me the one thing volunteers needed was empathy. No matter who they came across when on patrol, they needed to be able to empathise. It is likely they may not agree with what they've done or what they're going through, but empathy is crucial; negotiation can only work on that basis.

'Anything you can imagine really, we've had,' Ross said. 'We care for them, we're giving them a choice, other than ending their life.'

Ben's mobile phone had rung twice during the meeting. Both times he disappeared outside to answer it, and both times Ross looked up nervously while doing his best to continue to answer my questions. It must be like that every time the phone rings; who knows what it could be? Luckily each time Ben came back in after a minute or so and took his seat back on the settee, continuing with his mug of tea. Even so I knew my half hour was nearly over and I didn't want to take up too much of their time. I just had time to ask about the early days and what made Ross set up the team in the first place. Ben laughed, heartily. He'd obviously had to sit through this recounting of events before.

'I was a Christian minister,' Ross told me. 'At the time I was running a church and while praying one Sunday morning I really felt God was giving me a vision. It lasted about 30 minutes, and the closest I can explain is that it was like a daydream. But it was much more than that because I wasn't aware of time passing. It involved these two people patrolling Beachy Head and talking to those who were suicidal. In churches around Eastbourne we had prayed for these people and for this situation for a very long time. It's always very dangerous to pray about these things,' Ross said, chuckling to himself, 'in case God tells you you're the one who has to go and deal with it!'

I thought back to those statistics and to the small, wooden crosses with their inscriptions. Fifteen hundred lives saved. All because of a vision a man had in a church. The determination that Ross felt when he had this idea that, unlike so many others, he wouldn't just hope someone else would act on it. This wasn't a problem for others to deal with. It was something to dedicate your life to.

'From the moment the vision finished it was burning in my heart to set it up,' he continued. 'That was back in July 2003 and we started the following year, in August. I had a lot of shortcomings to overcome, for instance I don't like heights. A few of our team don't like heights but hopefully we don't get too close to the edge. The set-up was very complicated, we had to talk to the coastguards and the police and gather a team together and train them, raise the funds for basic equipment to get us working and all of that takes time. We needed to know that when we started we would be here for good. If you're going to say we will be here every day, you need to be there every day. If we were going to do it, it had to be done properly.'

Ross looked at his watch. Not in a rude way; sometimes people just need to know what time it is. He had told me he would have to rush off and I didn't want to delay him, so I thanked him and Ben for talking to me and put my mug on the side. Ross and Ben took their high-vis jackets from the pegs next to the door and we said our goodbyes. They set about their important business, while I went for a drink in the pub next door.

I sat with my beer and watched the videos I had recorded on my phone that afternoon. Beachy Head was such a beautiful place; even my shaky camerawork could not disguise that. I ordered another beer and felt relaxed for the first time that day, not just because I had met Ross and Ben but because I hadn't tumbled down the rocks when I was walking up there earlier. I am too clumsy to be an explorer and to stand at the edge of cliffs.

When I first entered the pub I still hadn't been able to relax completely, so intense was the reputation of Beachy Head. I knew the bar staff were trained as counsellors so that if there were ever troubled people in the pub, possibly there for their last meal, they could alert the Chaplaincy, and they'd know the right things to say, the way to behave. But I was surprised at how normal the pub seemed to be: chatty barmaid, locally brewed ales, roaring fire, steak night on Wednesdays, condom machines in the gents. I think in reality the pub perhaps attracted as many freelance journalists as it did suicidal people.

When I left the pub the pleasant afternoon had turned pitch black. Suddenly, Beachy Head was eerie. I'm not scared of the dark, but the lack of any light was terrifying. I think talking about death all day had affected my mind – my imagination was, for once, overactive, as a covering of clouds denied us the stars and the moon. There were no streetlamps, the only lights were those provided by the pub. It's a decent, pleasant walk by day to Eastbourne from Beachy Head, but suddenly it seemed insurmountable. I went back inside to ask the barmaid if she could give me a taxi number.

'They do such an important job,' the taxi driver told me when I said I'd spent the afternoon with the Chaplaincy Team. 'We have an emergency button we press if we have someone in our cab we are worried about. It goes straight to them. We have delaying tactics so that they can meet us at the destination. It's a beautiful part of the world, though. It's a shame we have this reputation.'

The taxi driver told me the reason he lived in Eastbourne was because when he was seven and his brother was eight, their mum was mugged outside their South London flat. She got in that evening and announced they were moving to Eastbourne where her sister lived. That was 20 years ago and he's never been back to London since. He's now got a seven-year-old of his own and loves living by the seaside, taking his daughter swimming in the sea in the summer.

'It's such a shame about this reputation,' he said again, shaking his head. 'Not a single person locally has a bad word to say about Eastbourne. Not even the students. They love it here. They're a lovely bunch.'

As the taxi continued back into Eastbourne, I thought about how the seaside is so full of eccentrics. People with metal detectors on the beach at 5am, or religiously playing on the 2p arcade machines, or all the families with their precise routines and traditions. But at the same time, seaside towns are full of people who go unnoticed. Like Ross and Ben. Sacrificing their time. Reaching out to people. Doing good deeds. Washing the Beachy Head patrol car. Making their corner of the world a safer place.

CHAPTER TWELVE

The Bird Droppings Conspiracy Theory

A burned down pier says so much about today's seaside. It's symbolic of something that was once loved, taken for granted, but has now disappeared. Except it hasn't disappeared, its relics are there for all to see. I was in Brighton, looking out at what used to be the West Pier. What was once beautiful was now cinder.

There is barely a pier in the UK that hasn't suffered from fire, vandalism, destruction or financial meltdown. Perhaps the most famous example in recent times is Hastings, first opened in 1872, the same year as the first statutory Bank Holiday. In his book *Pavilions on the Sea*, Cyril Bainbridge goes into detail about just how complex it was to construct those initial piers. Building a pier at Hastings had first been mentioned in 1861, but it took a decade for the idea to materialise. One of the main problems was opposition by local residents who feared it may be 'detrimental to the area of the borough by lowering its character as a place of fashionable resort'.

In 1990 Hastings Pier suffered storm damage, from which it never really recovered, forcing it to close in 1999. It reopened in 2002 but was soon sold off to an offshore enterprise, before being almost entirely destroyed by fire in 2010, a story much covered by the national news and provoking an incredible outpouring of sadness locally. Its story is far from unique. The theatre on Eastbourne Pier was destroyed by fire in January 1970, followed by hurricane damage in 1987. After serious corrosion damage in 1976, Bournemouth Pier had rebuilding costs of £1.7 million. Colywn Bay Pier has been closed since its former owner was made bankrupt in July 2008.

In 2006 Cleethorpes Pier was bought by local businessman Kash Pungi. In 2007, the new owner set to work on a five-month project to renew the pier's supporting legs, using over 40 tonnes of steel at an estimated cost more than £500,000. That same year the pier was granted a 24-hour drinking licence, but quickly serious crime and disorder marred the venue's reputation. Within three years the pier had gone into receivership and closed. A Grimsby-based businessman bought the pier for a six-figure sum, and pledged to restore it to its former glory. After a £200,000 upgrade it reopened in November 2010 with the promise that the pier would be made 'the envy of other resorts'. The new management introduced a dress code and stated that entry would be limited to over-21s. An Edwardian guidebook gives information about Cleethorpes Pier, stating that 'nimble visitors may revel in terpsichorean indulgence to their hearts' content'. Terpsichore was the Greek muse of dancing, the Pete Tong of his day. In 2012 the pier was once again on the market.

A slightly more charming story is that of Worthing Pier in 1913, when a gale-force wind hit the UK, affecting the pier. A brave audience of about 30 had settled down in the southern pavilion to a programme of light music by the McWhirter Quintet. Audience members started to leave to watch the force of nature that was the weather. The musicians wisely abandoned their music stands and, clutching their instruments, left the pier to watch the sightseers on the promenade.

Piers were vital during the war too: Birnbeck Pier at Weston-super-Mare was closed to the public and renamed HMS *Birkenhead*, and was used by scientists in the secret development of weapons; Llandudno pier was used for Home Guard training. As for Southend Pier, the playwright Sir Alan Herbert once said it should have been awarded the George Medal for its wartime services.

Piers have always had a secret life. If you go to a seaside town after sunset, it's towards the pier that the teenagers will gravitate. It's somewhere to feel rebellious, to plan and plot and work out your own place in the world. I am sure there are very few people who grew up in Brighton who don't have a story about a night under the pier.

Brighton is a seaside resort that has thrived while others have suffered. As early as the 18th century, George IV spent time there in what was considered a fashionable resort for those who liked cuisine and theatre.

Brighton continued to evolve as a much-loved holiday destination, and much later in its history was among the first to respond to the threat to British resorts from cheap holidays abroad: a key part of this was the opening of Brighton Conference Centre in 1974. Brighton has also reinvented itself with its pride in gay culture. In 2005 the first same-sex couple to legally tie the knot in a civil partnership came from Brighton.

While other resorts struggled, Brighton gained the reputation as one of the most important places in the UK, particularly for its love of culture and arts. It wasn't just artists, but media types, entrepreneurs and business owners who gravitated here. For anyone young and creative looking for somewhere to live, Brighton was the place to be. This had a knock-on effect: any new businesses opening also knew that Brighton would be a smart place to have their premises, so more and more people moved to the area. When the fast train connection to London was complete, Brighton had firmly established itself as a cool new place. Not only were there the creative people and culture, but also the seaside. The chip shops. The pebble beach. The pier.

Brighton once had three piers but now has just one. The Chain Pier was destroyed by storm in 1896. The Palace Pier suffered from severe fire damage in 2003 and the West Pier was damaged by both storm and fire, leading to its demolition in 2010. Today, the old Palace Pier (now just called Brighton

Pier) is the most visited pier in the UK and among the top ten visitor attractions in the country. I was meeting the person in charge, after pinging her a couple of speculative emails.

It had never really occurred to me that piers had managers. Shops have managers. Hotels have managers. Piers just float on the sea, as at home in the water as fish and plankton. I was intrigued to discover the inner workings of a pier. As I arrived for our scheduled meeting I hoped she might be able to give me tips on how to win on those 2p machines.

Neil, the lad on reception, told me that Mrs Martin was slightly delayed but she'd be with me as soon as she could. He asked if I'd like a coffee while I waited, and having just spent £2.20 on a disgusting hot dog I said yes, thinking in some way it balanced my costs. I'd wasted so much money on piers over the years it was about time I got something back. Neil brought over a mug of instant stuff, spied my notebook and asked, 'What's this all about, then?'

I said I was writing about piers and how they were so universal, so synonymous with the seaside, yet we don't really know much about them.

'Yes!' Neil replied. 'What are they? I've never really thought about that!'

'Like this room, for example,' I said. 'Who would have thought a pier would have a reception area with pot plants and a waiting room?'

It was as if the room existed on the offchance that someone would turn up one day claiming to be writing a book about the seaside.

'Are you going to write that we burned down the other two piers?' Neil asked with a laugh.

'I've been hearing some conspiracy theories about that,' I told him. The previous night in the pub when I told my friends I was staying with I was going to the pier, they told me some of the theories of how the West Pier had burnt down. Two guys in a motorboat had been seen zooming away from the fire in the dead of the night. Someone else told me that the owners couldn't afford to maintain the piers any longer and this was the quickest way to put an end to an increasingly unprofitable enterprise. No-one was ever charged with arson and it is still a bit of a mystery to locals – there were as many conspiracy theories as there were pebbles on the beach.

'No-one really knows what happened,' a man also in the waiting room told me. 'I think it was probably torched. No-one seems to know, though.'

At the back of the room one of Neil's colleagues, visible to me but not to young Neil, stepped forward. He worked in security. There was no uniform or badge to prove this, but then Elvis never wore a badge saying 'I am culturally significant.' There are some things we can work out for ourselves. His shoulders were wide enough to carry the weight of the whole pier.

'You want to know why that first pier burned down?' he asked. His voice carried a weight of authority, suggesting whatever he was about to say was the truth. 'Bird shit,' he continued. 'Before it burned down the pier was covered in thick bird shit. It had a glass roof, which acted as a magnifying glass. Eventually the sun heated the pier to such an extent that the whole place torched.'

'Bird shit?' asked Neil.

'Bird shit,' his colleague confirmed, definitively.

'Bollocks!' said Neil.

I was on Neil's side. Though that didn't stop me later researching whether or not bird droppings are flammable. I wasn't convinced this guy's theory was watertight, but my research backed up his theory. Bird mess, it turned out, is in fact incredibly flammable. Certain manures can be turned into dynamite, so, in theory, the pier absolutely could have been burned down as a result of bird droppings. It was still unlikely, though. Wasn't it?

'It trades on its history,' Mrs Martin told me once we were seated, each on a leather chair, in her plush office. I had asked her the main strengths of Brighton Pier. 'People are fond of the seaside and when you think of the seaside you think of piers. Most big seaside resorts have a pier of some sort. People come and have a look. Our pier is pretty unique, it's a third of a mile out to sea and there aren't that many seaside piers around any more, just 57 in the whole country, and most are nothing like this.'

I disagreed with this point slightly. All the piers I had visited, Southwold excepted, seemed to be treading the same ground. They were all pretty much identical, with their annoying music, stalls selling overpriced horrible-tasting sweets, hot dogs that taste of tins. Worst of all were the sticks of rock. I hate rock. It's horrible. Foul-tasting sticks of sugar. When you were at primary school your friend would always bring you back a stick of rock and you'd be so disappointed. Couldn't they have brought you back something more exciting, like a pencil sharpener or some stickers?

I told Mrs Martin that I had spent the last half hour wandering up and down the pier and asked her if she thought that was the way her pier would always be.

'It's what people expect to see,' she said, reclining into the cushioned back of her chair. 'It meets an expectation.'

As long as there are people around who connect with that British seaside feel then you'd be silly to change, because you're meeting the demand that's there.

'Some of it will never change,' she said, confidently. 'The rock shops and seafood bars have been here for a long time. There was a penny arcade here when the pier was first built. Candy floss has been here since 1946. We have a lot of the products that have been here since the beginning. We have fish that nibble your feet now, which is a bit more modern. We have arcades with videos. The products remain the same, but at the same time it is always evolving, always moving on.'

I had found the contact details for Mrs Martin when reading about a man who proposed to his girlfriend at Brighton Pier. I wanted to know more about the romance of piers – they are as much a narrative device as the clock at Waterloo Station or the Eiffel Tower. They attract eccentrics and bring out the eccentricities in otherwise normal people. That kind of thing happened all the time, Mrs Martin told me, very matter-of-fact. There wasn't even a hint of a twinkle in her eye. She said lots of people propose there.

People also want to get married there because it's where they first met, or where they got engaged.

It is also the place where people break up. I heard one story, possibly apocryphal, of a lady who made a living after pinpointing the place on Brighton Pier where ladies were most likely to throw off their wedding or engagement ring after an argument. She would regularly dive down, retrieve the rings and sell them to pay her rent.

The pier also has ceremonies where ashes are scattered. 'People in Brighton think of it as their pier even though it's been privately owned for 28 years. People I speak to in Brighton think of it as "our pier" but you wouldn't say "our Boots the Chemist", would you?'

'Or "our Millets",' I added, helpfully.

'Yes, and that's something we want to make sure continues. The Government preaches for "staycations" and to holiday in your own country, but VAT and tax laws make things very difficult for seaside businesses. If we are serious about re-creating the heyday of the British seaside we need to make sure our Government supports that with the correct measures to help seaside businesses. Hotels and shops need better support, and for that to happen the Government need to help, otherwise you'll see a decline. What distinguishes the seaside from other places is that they are made up of lots and lots of small businesses. You get the odd big hotel but the restaurants and the bars are small businesses and need encouragement. Piers are hugely expensive beasts to maintain because of the water. They require a huge amount of investment. In general I think we have maintained our pier well and invested in it sensibly. If you don't invest in it, it will die.'

I wasn't entirely convinced that the traditions Brighton Pier maintained were what people really wanted. At times traditions are overrated, too much importance can be placed on them. Overloading on tradition suggests being scared of the future. Maybe these traditions are things that as far as we know our grandparents at best tolerated. Where is the reinvention? Walking around the pier that afternoon I had found it frustrating. Brighton has so many visitors; many of them are bored, though. There's not really that much to do other than 'have a look around'. People want things to do. Or at least for that irritating music to stop.

After meeting Mrs Martin I decided to have one last walk up and down the pier. I'd only been to Brighton a couple of times. It was where my cool friends went to university, worked in trinket shops, were mates with the xylophone players of local bands. I spent time on the pier observing the day trippers, the tourists, the mismatch of people who constitute the pier's clientele on a chilly afternoon. I was particularly taken by two American girls, around my age. They were sitting on a bench, looking bored. Nearby was Brighton Pier Radio, whose sound system was competing with fairground waltzer music. The two girls got up and walked towards the exit.

'This music is ...' one of them said, the rest of the sentence disappearing into the English Channel. I don't think her next word was going to be 'ground-breaking', 'pivotal' or even 'bearable'. They looked so bored. They were shivering, each wearing at least two coats, and there was nothing

for them to do. It was then that I realised that piers can
be a bit shit. I'd arrived expecting to enjoy my time on
the pier, but I was disappointed. It wasn't much fun, boring
even, with irritating music, and was as much an anachronism
as insisting on being addressed as 'Mrs Martin'. The Palace
Pier was more like a monument to a bygone era than a place
of entertainment.

Another part of the seaside's bygone age is the lido. While
Brighton Pier may be one of 57 such remaining structures,
the number of seaside lidos has dwindled to just a handful.
In fact, there are only three of them left in the country and
it was feared that one of those, at neighbouring Saltdean,
might not be around for much longer.

The first seaside lido in the UK opened in Skegness in
1932, followed by Penzance in 1935, and Morecambe the
following year. Dozens more followed, the councils of each
seaside town competing to come up with something more
inventive and modern with the design of their pools or
buildings or decking. When Britain was at peace after the
War lidos were finally allowed to prosper. They were vibrant,
animated, a sign of post-War stoicism, of people enjoying
their freedom.

Saltdean was established in the 1930s by Charles Neville,
who had a vision to set up second homes there. He was
travelling nearby on the way to a holiday in Eastbourne
when he saw all the flat land. This gave him the idea to do

something with the area. He built Saltdean from scratch, as he had done earlier with nearby Peacedean, planting trees and building houses and roads. Neville displayed eccentricities not dissimilar to Billy Butlin, whose attempts to buy the lido he always prevented. Neville once set up a raffle with a newly built house in Saltdean worth £1,000 as a prize. He sold tickets, 766 of which were blank but one of which had the word *House* written on it. The raffle was won by a lady called Agnes.

As Saltdean grew, the lido became its heart and hub: it is said that Billy Butlin wanted to buy the lido, and build cable cars between it and his hotel. Even during the enforced break caused by the War the lido was still active: the premises became a training ground for the fire brigade, who pumped water from the pool. This had repercussions, though, and by the end of the War the main pool was in a poor state with tiles dropping off, despite barely having been used by the public for swimming.

Since then the lido had a turbulent history and has been closed more than it has been open. Recently, though, a group of people had taken action, determined that Saltdean wouldn't be yet another seaside town admitting defeat, allowing lidos to exist only in folklore. It was Rebecca, one of the group's campaigners, whom I'd come to Saltdean to see.

I had been in Saltdean for an hour, wandering around on the seafront and in the town. There wasn't a lot to do other than slip on the seaweed on the rocks. It was hard to believe the area was once thriving. I made my way to the Saltdean Tavern, where I was meeting Rebecca. Inside, a pensioner at the bar queried the coupon he was using: 'I do get a pudding, do I? It says I am entitled to a pudding. It's my birthday.'

The barman read and reread the coupon before deciding that yes, he was allowed a birthday pudding. Content with the news, the pensioner dangled his walking stick over his arm and carried the tray of four pints of tap water to his three friends at the table next to mine. As he did so Rebecca arrived. I waved a hello in her direction, recognising her because of the Save Saltdean Lido cloth bag she was carrying.

Rebecca told me about the history of the lido, and also that of Saltdean itself. She pointed in the direction of where the Grand Ocean Hotel played host to film stars and royalty in the 1930s. The Art Deco hotel with its 426 rooms opened in 1937, all glitz and glamour, sea views and a resident orchestra. It was described as a 'continental-style seaside resort hotel with glass-enclosed sun-decks – a sunbather's paradise'. But, as was becoming the theme with seasides across the UK, this could not last. In 1972 the hotel was sold, and has changed hands several times since, until December 2004 when it closed for the final time.

'Our doctor's surgery is now on the ground floor,' she told me, 'so it is a very grandiose trip to the doctors. It's nice that old buildings can be put to good use.'

Rebecca explained how in the 1960s Brighton Council had tried to buy the lido to make it a community facility, but Charles Neville refused to sell it, demanding a ludicrously high amount of money in return. It was when Neville died in 1960 that the opportunity arose for the Council to buy it. They built an extension that included a library and a community centre. By the end of the late 1990s it was in a pretty poor state of repair, and the Council decided it didn't want the liability of running the pool any more. They sold off the piece of land, which included the Saltdean Tavern where we were sitting, to Marlborough Leisure. That money went into restoring the lido and on necessary maintenance work.

This is where Dennis Audley entered the story, one of the Marlborough directors who had taken over the lease. It is he whom the campaigners were battling with. Rebecca, a lovely and patient lady, was clearly angered at just having to say his name out loud.

'Last year Mr Audley held a public meeting to announce his plans to fill the pool with concrete and build seven storeys on top of the existing building to create 800 flats,' Rebecca told me. His plans were met with outrage, not just because people didn't want the flats but because architecturally this is a special building.

Rebecca told me that local people were so unhappy by all of this that a group got together and decided to start a campaign, and come up with some solutions. Rebecca and six or seven other like-minded Saltdean folk set up a committee and formed the Save Saltdean Lido campaign, which has gone from strength to strength: they put in the listing application for Grade II* status, which was subsequently granted; they developed a business plan and started working with Sir Terence Conran and his architectural practice, who supported the campaign; they'd started funding applications to the Heritage Lottery Fund and were putting a lot of pressure on the council to try and get things resolved.

Rebecca took a poster out of her cloth bag, unrolled it. 'If you drive around Saltdean every house has one of these in their front window. Everyone knows about it, we all want the lido to be saved.'

I wasn't surprised. Rebecca's passion was infectious. A couple of days earlier I'd never heard of Saltdean or its lido, but now the thought of it closing down and being replaced with flats horrified me. It stated clearly in the lease that the pool was supposed to be open every day from the end of May until the beginning of September but the campaigners had compiled a daily log, which revealed that the previous summer it had been open for just 43 days. Other lidos were open every day without fail. If you are running a business you need to be consistent and reliable. People would travel a long way to find the lido closed on a glorious day.

Rebecca and her fellow campaigners had spoken to 3,000 local residents and 500 tourists about the lido. The feedback they got was substantial: the water was freezing cold; the children's play area was taken away a number of years ago, as were the tables and chairs, and there were no lockers. There was a gym, but there were buckets of water across the floor because the roof was leaking. Who was going to go on a treadmill when there was water splashing around everywhere? There were no curtains in the showers in the changing rooms. It was like a boarding school from the dark ages. A lot of the feedback was that people didn't want to use it because it wasn't very nice. It wasn't exactly an inviting proposition. You couldn't get hot food or alcohol. There was nothing there to really make you want to stay.

'This is a fight worth fighting,' Rebecca told me, sipping her fizzy water. 'People across the world have been in contact with their support, people who had met their wives or husbands there. Some who had been with their parents, learnt to swim there or had taken their children there. We've lost too many of these lidos.'

Saltdean is the only Grade II* listed lido in the country, which makes it the most important lido left. The Saltdean campaigners were determined that their hard work would preserve it for future generations, while retaining that charm of the 1930s.

'It just made me so angry to read about the plans for the lido's future,' Rebecca continued. 'Audley came back a month later and said that he had revised his plans, and now he just wanted 70 flats instead. The community pointed out to him that we don't want any flats! We wanted a lido and if it was being run properly we could use it. The place is so run down, John!' she said, shaking her head. 'But now that the building is Grade II* listed it means no-one can touch it.'

'You're winning!'

'Maybe,' Rebecca said, cautiously.

Rebecca talked positively about the future. The campaigners had presented the most signed local petition ever to the local Council, with all 55 members of the Council voting in favour of supporting the campaign and for legal action to commence. It seemed it was an achievable goal to have a functioning, vibrant lido, just like in 1937. There were plans to put in a dance studio, renovate the gym, have an ice-skating rink, incorporate farmers' markets, weddings, arts and crafts.

When it was designed in the 1930s the lido had community at its heart. This was a chance to bring that back again.

The two other active seaside lidos were in Plymouth and in Grange-over-Sands in Cumbria. Both were experiencing similar problems and also had campaigns in place to preserve something so vital to the seaside. English Heritage had granted the Art Deco Grange lido listed status after the land was purchased by a local businessman to turn it into a medical centre and housing. A spirited group of campaigners had been doing what the Saltdean team had been involved with, all for the good of their community.

Rebecca unravelled a roll of photographs. 'It's such a part of our heritage,' she said, showing me pictures of how the lido used to be. 'With these buildings, it's the case that once they're gone, they're gone. And that's part of our seaside culture disappeared forever. They will never be replaced, no-one is going to say, "Ooh, we should build a lido."'

The campaign estimated they could restore the lido at a cost of around 3.5 million pounds, not a huge amount of money when it comes to restoration. In theory, they would attract people who wouldn't otherwise have come to the area to visit the restored, flourishing lido. People would talk about it, word of mouth would travel: 'Have you heard about Saltdean lido? It's up and running again and better than ever!' Architecturally it's significant. It still has the original stair turrets up to the balcony. You can imagine sitting there with a drink, looking out.

'It should be an asset,' Rebecca said as we put our coats on ready to head outside, 'rather than something slightly embarrassing that can't be used, not being utilised.'

'Yet another boarded-up building.'

'It's not good,' she agreed. 'It has an impact on the local area and on other local businesses.'

The people in the Saltdean Tavern quibbling over their vouchers would have remembered the early days of the lido. Standing in the car park, it was easy to imagine what this place must have been like in the 1960s and that it could easily happen again. A fully functioning lido would do wonders for the area, for the reputation of seaside towns across the UK. Maybe it would cause other councils to think again, maybe get their hammers and pliers out and get rid of the planks of wood boarding up the lidos, and make our seaside towns vibrant again.

'People want to teach their children to swim at the lido', Rebecca said, 'just as they were taught by their parents. People like the security of the lido. There are no worries of drifting out to sea in a dinghy.'

It was cold outside the pub, words were coming out of our mouths with their own vapour trails. Anyone swimming outdoors in this weather would be covered in goose pimples and have to take the next day off school. But in the summer, families would visit in their thousands.

As we exchanged goodbyes I told Rebecca how much I loved what she was doing and the plans the group had for the lido. A smile glowed above her scarf and buttoned-up coat.

When I was by myself again I went for another look around before heading back to Brighton, and again I could hear the screams and the splashing around of the 1960s. It was so sad it wasn't used to its potential. Rebecca had told me about the enthusiastic press coverage they had received; that Sandi Toksvig had interviewed them for Radio 4 and had asked to be invited back once their campaign had proved to be a success, as it inevitably would be. It was so important that these people were fighting this fight. Good people backing a good cause. We all worry about a lack of community, and what better way to enjoy shared experiences than a massive outdoor swimming pool?

I love tradition, it's crucial; I like cassette tapes and posting letters, but at the same time I am lost when my wireless connection goes down or if I can't find somewhere to charge up my iPad. Surely piers could have a nod towards the past, but was it so necessary to wallow in it? The lido seemed to be embracing the future, whereas I knew people who had lived in Brighton for years who had been surprised when I told them I was going to the pier. But happily it seemed that the Save Saltdean Lido campaign was going well. A few months after my visit it was announced on the Save Saltdean Lido website that the Council had negotiated an agreement with the leaseholder and will be taking back ownership of the lease. Rebecca told the BBC website: 'We're completely overwhelmed. We can't believe it's actually happened.'

Before we knew it Sandi Toksvig and I could be on our sun loungers, sipping posh cocktails as people of all generations splashed around in the pool, parents teaching their kids how to swim.

CHAPTER THIRTEEN

The Saucy Postcard
Museum

'You have to come!' James Bissell-Thomas, owner of the Donald McGill saucy postcard museum in Ryde, had urged me over the phone. 'It's so special here. It's a lovely little room, we're all so proud of what we have here.'

I had phoned him because I wanted to know more about his collection of saucy seaside postcards.

'You have to see it to understand,' he maintained, and I knew that it wouldn't be long before we were standing in the same room. I decided that a combination of my family history and saucy postcards meant I would make the journey to the Isle of Wight. I got to go on a hovercraft! For those who lived there, and in similar places, such a trip would be a fairly routine journey, but for me getting a hovercraft was the highlight of my month.

As I arrived at Southsea station the sun was out, so I walked the couple of miles to the hovercraft terminal. Even then, I still had time before I had to depart, so I went to a café to get some lunch. A banner with the words 'FA Cup Final 2008' emblazoned across it was hanging high behind the counter, despite the fact that Portsmouth had been relegated and were now fighting for survival. The image of Portsmouth as a successful football team seemed as rooted to the past as all the exhibits at the D-Day museum across the seafront. A waitress was reminiscing with a customer about a dinosaur ride that used to be on the esplanade: 'I asked for my money back last time I was on it,' she said, the disappointment still evident. 'That was five years ago, probably. Maybe 15.'

Both were around the same age as me; it was alarming that for all of us even decades were now becoming hard to distinguish. It made me realise that what I thought was a few years since my last visit to the Isle of Wight was actually almost 20 years ago. I had been to the Isle of Wight once before and wanted to revisit some of those places on the island we had been to that time. The places from which I'd sent postcards as a 12-year-old:

Dear Grandma. Having a nice holiday. Love from John.

Dear Grandma. It is sunny. Love from John.

Dear Grandma. We are on holiday. Love from John.

There are other crossings possible to the Isle of Wight by ferry, but hovercraft is the quickest way to get to the island. It takes ten minutes to cross the Solent, although I certainly wasn't in any rush. On the television in the corner of the terminal the BBC News 24 channel was broadcasting live footage of David Cameron and Nick Clegg arriving at a tractor factory in Basildon to address the press about recent budget cuts. A less inspiring sentence I can't imagine. A few seats away from me a lady made a phone call trying to rearrange a doctor's appointment, battling through the automated voice system. I had thought the whole idea of living on the Isle of Wight was slightly strange and exotic, but it really isn't. For many people getting a ferry is as routine as catching a bus or bleeping in your Oyster card and waiting for the Central Line.

I picked up a copy of the free Isle of Wight magazine. I read that by the year 2020 the Isle of Wight planned to have become completely self-sufficient in energy, food, water and fuel. Power for the population of 142,500 could come from a waste-to-energy plant, solar panels, and tidal and geothermal power. Eco Island founder, David Green, said 'The island is taking some of its destiny back into its own hands.'

By the time I finished the article we were boarding. A man in a smart uniform had climbed a ladder and the safety announcements were being made. All the staff were being very blasé about the whole thing: it was almost like they did it every day. But I was different. At no point while visiting seaside towns had I been as excited as at that moment. If the seaside is all about escapism, what better way to get away from your day-to-day life than on a hovercraft?

Once on the Isle of Wight I began my visit by walking along Ryde Beach. There was a fenced-off playground, sand cushioning the fall of the toddlers of the island. A toddler in a summer dress was screaming with disappointment because her parents were telling her it was time to go home. They were a cruel couple, denying this little girl the opportunity to play on the swings forever. Hopefully they compensated her with fish fingers for tea.

A notice board promoted various local activities. In crayon bubble writing was an advertisement for trampolining. 'Children can have fun with a perfect outlet for energy and at the same time develop co-ordination and control that is so important for healthy growth and development.' The poster for Ryde deckchairs, meanwhile, simply said, 'Why just stand … when you can sit?'

I was enjoying being back at the seaside. I took my shoes off. Put on the flip-flops I'd brought specially with me in my rucksack. After 20 minutes I was pretty tired. I was wearing a big jumper and had a heavy bag on. If you look at any professional athlete, anyone doing a marathon or the steeplechase, you'll notice they're not wearing big jumpers. They don't have heavy bags. It's one of the first things you learn at athletics school.

Particularly bustling was Ryde Marine Bowls Club, where a game was taking place: Ryde Ladies versus Warner Ladies. A spattering of family members were sitting on benches watching. There was polite applause and murmurs of encouragement. 'Come on Grandma!' a cajoled little boy shouted. Next to the game there were greens open to the public, where you could hire bowls from the kiosk.

There was a paperback book sale: 50p for a John Grisham. Everything in Ryde seemed to take on a new simplicity. As I walked along the seafront a coach trip arrived; pensioners descended to start their holiday. Hopefully Ryde had enough tonic water to cater for them.

Just beyond the beach was a funfair. Spinning teacups, a helter-skelter. A boating lake. Are there two words in the English language that fit as well together as 'boating lake'? Lennon McCartney, possibly. Fresh bread. Paddling pool. Apple crumble. Free bar. Maybe there's quite a lot of them.

The Donald McGill Postcard Museum was just a couple of minutes from the hover terminal, and to get there you passed several newsagents, all of them selling McGill merchandise. The rudest had been reprinted as T-shirts, mugs, posters. There was smut everywhere in Ryde. All the little shops had got 'Stick of Rock cock' memorabilia, like it was Man United or Justin Bieber. The most notable image was the boy with a huge piece of rock reaching into the sky from his pants with the headline *Stick of rock, cock?*

I walked up Union Street and stopped off at the café at the museum's entrance. A model of Earth hung from the ceiling and around it were all the planets, which moved accurately in relation to one another. It was very *Blue Peter*. If you put a pound in the machine it lit up and rotated while the rest of the café got on with their tea and scones. The waitress could have been straight out of a Two Ronnies sketch. She seemed overawed at the fact that there were three customers who had all arrived at around the same time. I ordered, she told me to sit down and she brought me over a hot chocolate, then a jacket potato, then a glass of Diet Coke before she got my order right.

There was an admission charge of £3.50 to get into the museum. On the phone James had explained to me that this meant anyone going in knew what they were going in for, what they were going to get. 'Any complaints we get are generally that it isn't smutty enough,' he told me. The people James wanted coming to his museum were art students and lovers of the English language: McGill's play on words is delightful to witness. Predominately, though, they get people who remember the cards. An older clientele. That was certainly the case judging by the people in the café, and when I paid and went through the turnstile the only two people there were a couple who looked like they were in their 70s. They were, like me, craning their necks to see a staggering sight: 2,600 postcards were stuck to the ceiling of the museum, apparently in chronological order. The museum was just one small room and there wasn't a single lick of paint that wasn't covered by a postcard or memorabilia relating to McGill. Rarely had I been so overwhelmed to be in a room. I walked round and realised what James had meant when he had urged me to come and visit.

'Hello John!' he said, walking through the door marked Private. It was James I had been looking forward to meeting as much as seeing his museum, so engaging and passionate had he been when we spoke on the phone. James explained how he came to be running a postcard museum: 'Originally it was going to be a globe museum,' he told me. James was one half of Greaves & Thomas, the UK's sole commercial globe makers ('reviving the art of traditional globe making').

'Then one day I thought about doing a one-off saucy postcard marquee at the bottom of the Esplanade. In doing my research I came across this guy Donald McGill time and time again. I didn't really know of him, but I found out that he was the one, the champion of all postcards.'

It was this fascinating history that made the museum such an attractive addition to Ryde's tourist board. In 1953, five shops in the town were raided by the police and had their postcards seized. In one shop the police left with 12 postcards, in another shop, 3,000. These were such exciting discoveries, a whole new world completely unknown to me was suddenly there to be explored. James managed to buy the copyright and build up a very substantial collection.

'What we have here in Ryde is the backbone of everything of his that exists, including a book he wrote which was never published at the time.'

It wasn't just James who was fascinated by Donald McGill. *Punch* magazine described him as 'the most popular, hence most eminent English painter of the century'. Dennis Potter called him 'Picasso of the Pier'. Ronnie Barker acknowledged these saucy postcards as one of the biggest influences on his comedy. In Ronnie Corbett's memoir, *And It's Goodnight From Him*, he recalled two characters they played in *The Two Ronnies*: the long-haired Country and Western duo Jehosophat and Jones. Corbett remembered that their lyrics, written by Barker, were 'often unashamedly influenced by the McGill postcards that he loved so much'.

Ronnie Barker was a collector of a vast array of things, but most notable was his love of postcards. He had a collection of 53,000, some so valuable they had to be stored in vaults. This led the Two Ronnies to make a silent film called *By the Sea*. Ronnie Corbett described it as 'the seaside postcard brought to life, his tribute to the world of McGill ... probably, therefore, his most personal work of all'. The film proved to be as controversial as the postcards that inspired him so much. Corbett recalled that infamous broadcast standards campaigner Mary Whitehouse complaining about two scenes in particular, one in which 'the delightful Madge Hindle, acting as companion to a rather grand lady played by Barbara New, lingered rather too long over a rack of postcards on the pier, and got a sharp prod from the grand lady's parasol for her pains'. Mary Whitehouse claimed that these scenes were 'encouraging violence'.

James, like Ronnie Barker, saw Donald McGill in a rather different light to Mary Whitehouse. One thing he was keen to clarify was that his man Donald McGill was not simply a man responsible for creating smut.

McGill's career started by accident. In 1904, when he was 30, he sent a cartoon to his nephew in hospital. It showed a man up to his neck in a frozen pond. The caption read 'Hope you get out!' It was just to make the little boy laugh, but ended up being forwarded to a publisher who commissioned his work.

'That,' James continued, 'is a better representation of his work than the ladies on the beach in swimming costumes. People expect to see nothing but saucy cards, but that's where the beauty of Mr McGill lies. He did everything from shopkeeping to fashion, motoring, invention, crosswords, telegrams, Christmas cards. He just looked at a slice of society from a comical eye. His postcards are very special and clever and subtle, with *double entendres*. They're showing something that only the mature eye can see.'

At the museum's opening party, with McGill's grandson Patrick Tumber present, a vicar interrupted proceedings, protesting, saying it was all in bad taste and asking everyone to leave. It turned out to just be a member of staff dressed up, a joke played on those in attendance. But while those working at the museum could see the funny side, others were taking more convincing. Shortly after the museum opened, James had found himself expressing exasperation at the legacy of the postcards in an interview with the *Isle of Wight County Press*. 'Donald McGill remained a modest man and, in my opinion, he never really received the recognition he deserved.'

'One of the things I love about McGill is that he wasn't afraid to have alternative ideas,' James continued as I followed him around the museum. 'His politics were very liberal. He freely admitted he was an atheist. That really wasn't a popular stance in those days. Look at these,' he urged me, beckoning me towards one of the displays. The postcards were of ladies marching.

'The Suffragette colours were white, green and purple,' he explained. 'You see McGill use these colours over and over again. He's definitely giving this old lady a Suffragette costume, implying that no-one will want her because she is a little spinsterish woman, that no-one will want her because she's capable of these independent thoughts. The same with this picture,' he said, pointing at another. 'A big, tubby woman in purple and green. It's a recurring theme. He's using every aspect of his art to bring these thoughts into public consciousness. The Scotsmen cards are a bit of fun too, a little boy being told by his dad, "Don't let the ball bounce more than once or you'll wear it out."'

McGill was certainly a fascinating character. Due to a rugby accident at the age of 16 he had had to have his right foot amputated. This meant he couldn't join up and serve his country in the First World War. During the war years he tried harder than ever to produce and design cards with a patriotic theme. One example is two neighbours talking over the fence: 'The war'll be over in a fortnight now, 'cos my ole man's joined the army an' I know 'e never keeps a job longer than that.' Many of the cards, though, were just about life. A man smiling with a frothy beer says 'It's better to be alive with 18 pence than dead with a thousand pounds.'

At every display case James stopped and enthusiastically explained the significance of each piece, the importance of the display culturally and politically. Others who were browsing in the museum were clearly enjoying a unique guided tour as I followed James around, scribbling notes as he talked quickly and passionately, without taking a breath, partly as he was so enthusiastic about his subject but also partly because he had a train to catch.

'Here are the banned cards,' he told me in a corner of the room. 'They were so strict! In the Isle of Man, any postcard which showed a vicar was automatically banned. How ridiculous! Even if it was a vicar waving hello, it would be banned because it was a possible source of detrimental thoughts towards the church. Look at this one, for example.'

He showed me one card, a little boy and little girl, both in their swimming costumes, and the girl is saying 'Just wait until you get into the sea.'

'Obviously in our perverted minds it's because he's going to have a wee in the sea. But it might not mean that! It could mean, "Just wait until you get into the sea … it's going to be fantastic!" Then there's this one alongside. "You girls don't know what the doctor's got in his bag for you."

'I still can't see what that would mean!' James said to me, genuinely baffled. 'Is it contraception? Is it an abortion kit? I've studied it and still can't tell the joke! Yet it was banned! It's just really bizarre.'

Of the 21 cards that were banned, 17 had to be withdrawn after the existing print run had gone. With the remaining four they had to cease publication and be burned. One that is particularly rude is a girl pointing at a baby boy in the bath, saying, 'It isn't a whistle, I've tried.' That is admittedly a pretty graphic one. But the 1857 Obscene Publications Act stated that if it was an image that would corrupt a minor then it would be deemed obscene. This is classic McGill: innocent picture, innocent text, it's only our minds that make it rude. He isn't doing anything against the Obscene Publications Act. The Donald McGill story, published in-house at the museum, recalls his statement through his lawyers: 'I had no intention of "double meaning" and, in fact, a "double meaning" was in some cases later pointed out to me.' It's only because he pleaded guilty that it went through. If he had pleaded innocent he would never have been sentenced.

McGill was 79 years old when the trial took place in Lincoln in 1954, the result of a letter a vicar had written about some of the postcards he had seen were for sale. The prosecution meant a loss of reputation, the destruction of a lot of his artwork and thousands of pounds of lost revenue.

'That was Donald having a senior moment,' James said to me, genuinely moved by the fact that this was realistically the moment McGill's career ended. 'He was an old man and he wrongly agreed to plead guilty. He was given bad advice. It's a tragedy for him and his company. It was a big loss. Such a bad feeling. A sad day.'

I asked James if he had a favourite card.

'I'm very fond of *The It Girl*,' he told me. This was one I had noticed as being particularly rude, a glamorous lady in a red dress and high heels, with two men looking at her across the road. The text reads, *She's a nice girl. Doesn't drink or smoke, and only swears when it slips out!*

'She was published in 1936,' James told me about the card, of which he had an almost life-size cardboard cut-out. 'When this card was being printed, whether it was pre-War, during the War, afterwards, there were no problems. But then in 1953 she started getting burned in every town. She was in more trouble than the *Stick of rock, cock*.'

It was quite funny to hear such terminology being used in a very serious way. '*Stick of rock, cock* had seven orders of destruction, but this was deemed prostitution,' James told me. He showed me the piece of paper with the places that had ordered its destruction. 'Penzance, order of destruction. Torquay, order of destruction. There's ten! In 1957, they tried to take her to trial but she was acquitted. So she's been through the mill. And because it's such a clever card with a *double entendre* it's perfect, it really is one of McGill's best. It's colloquial speech: you don't even see the *double entendre* at first, it's just brilliant and it really sums him up.'

While I was looking at the displays James would occasionally approach other visitors.

'Are you enjoying the museum?' he asked a lady reading the postcards.

'I love it!' she told him. 'I had no idea it was here. I've come here with my mother for a couple of days away. We've been here for two days and we feel so lucky we've stumbled across it. I saw a link online when I was looking for train times. So I said, well, the weather's not too good, let's have a look at these postcards.'

James showed me a couple of other special cards with stories attached, then apologised, telling me he had to leave to catch his train. He encouraged me to stay for as long as I liked and I could quite happily have stayed overnight and still wouldn't have got anywhere near viewing the entire collection on display. James could barely have left the island before a man with a thick Yorkshire accent approached me.

'If you're writing about postcards, you've got to check out this guy James Bamforth,' he said to me. 'To my mind, he's superior to McGill. I used to work for the factory in Holmfirth, Yorkshire. It's a listed building, but it's going to rack and ruin. All the windows are broken and it breaks my heart to see. He produced very similar things to McGill.'

James Bamforth, it transpired, started producing postcards in 1910 and by 1960 Bamforth Postcards had become the world's largest publisher of comic postcards. There were four staff artists who contributed the bulk of the output, and freelance artists were occasionally used.

The 50,000 images from the Bamforth collection are now owned by a man called Ian Wallace who explained his love of these postcards to the *Metro*. 'They always look good and they always make people smile,' he said. 'Maybe they're not to everyone's taste but if you can't laugh at Bamforth postcards what can you laugh at?' Wallace continued, 'All we're hearing about at the moment is cuts, cuts, cuts. It's good to have something we can all laugh about.'

But no matter what whispering Yorkshiremen might say, there is only one true producer of saucy postcards. If Donald McGill is good enough for James and for Ronnie Barker, then he's good enough for me, and to show my loyalty I now drink my cups of tea from a *Stick of rock, cock* mug.

The most fascinating side of McGill's life was not the smut or the banned cards, it was something much simpler. He had a love of anthropology. He believed 'it gave one a sense of perspective'. During a magazine interview, talking on the subject he said, 'it makes you realise you are no more than a blade of grass'. He is now buried in an unmarked grave within a private family plot in Streatham Cemetery. Towards the end of his life he is reported to have summed it up by saying, 'I am not proud. I had hoped to do something better.'

The thought of him feeling unfulfilled was a sobering one. McGill achieved something so few do, making him a true artist in that he will be remembered forever. The response of people telling James how much they were enjoying his museum was proof enough of that. My favourite postcard of his was a father saying to his son, 'You're getting a big boy now and I want to have a talk with you about the facts of life.'

'Okay Dad,' the son replies. 'What is it you want to know?'

CHAPTER FOURTEEN

F'Hutima Whutbread and Friends

I was in Bournemouth, voted Number One beach in the UK by TripAdvisor users, and it is a braver person than me to dispute them. I had combined my visit with a day working at the university and, as was now second nature, once completed I ended up heading down to the sea.

I walked past the beach huts, units along the promenade there to 'prettify a functional walkway'. These were carefully colour co-ordinated, lilacs to blues to purples to greens like a case of neatly laid-out coloured pencils. A blue plaque was above the door of one with the words *Bournemouth Beach Bungalow. Constructed 1909. First municipal beach hut in the UK in 1909.*

In recent years it was Southwold that had been synonymous with beach huts. The press enjoyed printing details of the rise in costs at the upper-middle-class resort, most notably when Gordon Brown chose it as his holiday destination when he was Prime Minister. But it was Bournemouth that had the history when it came to beach huts.

There are, according to Bournemouth Borough Council, around 20,000 beach huts in the UK. They evolved from bathing machines, first used in 1753. These were huts on wheels pulled along the beach by a horse, often carrying sick people to be restored by the fabled health benefits of the water. Inside the hut you would get changed and be dropped into the sea. As so many people who visited the sea were doing so for health reasons, being transported by horses and wheels was their only option to get close to the sea to be dunked in the water, bringing them back to full health.

Bathing machines evolved with different designs and sizes and colours into what we now see as a traditional beach hut. They have continued to evolve in recent years. Most notable were the new state-of-the-art beach pods in Boscombe. I found these pods completely by accident. As so often happened at the seaside, you lose track of time, and without realising it I had left Bournemouth beach behind me and was two miles down the road in Boscombe. This was a resort which flourished between the Wars but had suffered subsequently, particularly with drugs problems in the 1990s. Now, however, it was reinventing itself through its pier and its beach huts: the resort had the UK's first purpose-built, fully disabled-accessible beach huts and was also home to these beach pods, chic and spacious. The beach huts were dusty paperbacks, these were Kindles. The kind of place you expect film directors and record producers to hang out with the kind of people who call themselves mixologists. They look like a trendy minimalist New York bookstore that just stocks a few copies of the new Douglas Coupland novel, an obscure anthology edited by Dave Eggers and a copy of *French Vogue*. The nice thing about beach huts was that they were just that – huts. They'd be personified with a lick of paint, maybe a mural of a donkey, a seaside-related pun as a name: 'Life's a Beach.' These pods seem more like places to recharge your MacBook than somewhere to make a cup of tea. During peak time, the end of June to the first week of September, these pods cost £250 a week to hire, or £2,000 for the whole summer. Alternatively you could buy a ten-year lease for £17,995.

The pod experiment was headed up by Hemingway Designs, founded by Wayne and Geraldine Hemingway in 1981, which focused on 'affordable and social design, with a core philosophy of aiming to improve things that matter in life'. According to the *Bournemouth Echo* in 2010, their eye-catching retro design has impressed industry experts and helped to make Boscombe an award-winning resort.

'It's not often,' Wayne Hemingway explained on the Boscombe website, 'you come across a historic mid-century modern building that's been empty for 15 years, but has remained in good condition and has its original features and integrity. And when that building faces one of

Britain's best beaches, has world-class views and is next to one of the coolest piers in the country, you have to pinch yourself.'

Hemingway said he and his wife were very fond of the area. The National Pier Society awarded Boscombe Pier of the Year in 2010, an impressive achievement as the pier seemed to contain so little, just a few benches and a dustbin. It provided quite a stark contrast to the piers back in Brighton and Southwold.

I'd been lucky enough to get in touch with Wayne Hemingway, and had told him over the phone how I was fascinated with his involvement in the seaside. I knew he was patron of Morecambe Winter Gardens and clearly he had a long association with the beach.

'The seaside has had a big influence on me,' he told me over the phone. 'My nan was always dancing on Morecambe pier, my mum was always at the seafront. Morecambe was a pretty cool place in the 60s. I learned to ride my bike along the seafront. I went fishing, I spent a lot of time at the mussel beds. That was my life, really. When we first had kids we used to weekend at West Wittering, the closest sandy beach to London. We'd stay in B&Bs and eventually bought a house there.'

I asked Wayne about the beach pods project in Boscombe. He explained how it combined his love of the seaside with his passion for mid-century modern architecture: 'There was a block of beach pods, for want of a better word, that had seen better days, and it was pretty obvious a generation of people who enjoy mid-century modern architecture could cherish that place. It's a prime location, nice food, surf shops, and it's next to a sandy beach and the lovely pier. It seemed a no-brainer to work with the Council on it. It won Regeneration Scheme of the Year. From being an unloved part of wider Bournemouth it is quite clearly becoming massively popular.'

Hemingway seemed very reluctant to use the word 'pod' when we spoke. He spat it out like a bad olive and I can't say that I blamed him, but it seems an appropriate, if unappetising, description for his invention.

'Boscombe Beach looks fantastic. When you're there it feels like you're in Los Angeles or Venice Beach. It's become a really cool place to hang out. It's good to be involved in an aesthetic, to be involved with memorabilia. That gives you a head start – if it's something that means something passionate to you, it means you'll do a better job. We don't treat it as just a job, it means something deep down.'

I could see what he meant as I walked along Boscombe seafront, the sun bright in the sky, a man with his top off on rollerblades, his dog on his lead running alongside him, a couple hand in hand sharing a Calippo. I had a look at what I'd be able to buy if I had the inclination to spend a few grand on a beach pod. Hut 226, named for functionality rather than romance, was available.

In Southwold the beach huts all have names: 'Robin's Nest', 'The Look Out', 'Just Perfick'. In Sandown they are all puns based on famous people, alongside spurious facts relating to beach huts. 'Sir Len Hutton' – who made his highest score of 999 not out (then the tide came in). 'Margaret Beck-hutt'. 'F'hutima Whutbread'. 'Alfred Hutchcock', who was attacked on Sandown beach by hundreds of seagulls, giving him the idea for the film *The Birds*. They went on and on, although I stopped reading them after 'Ronnie Corb-hut'. I have a very low threshold for puns.

Hut 226 was a second-floor single beach pod with four director's chairs, two deckchairs, a windbreak, a table and electricity. They are more like trendy flats than what you would traditionally associate with a beach hut and they really represented the modernisation of the area.

The beach pods, however, had not been quite as successful as perhaps had been expected. I was disappointed to learn this, a few weeks after having spent time admiring the pods on the sunny day in Boscombe and speaking to Hemingway, who had been so enthusiastic about his design. According to the *Bournemouth Echo*, sales had been disappointing, with agents Savills and Goadsby selling just 12 pods between them. 'To be honest, we didn't really receive a lot of enquiries,' one estate agent was quoted as saying by the paper. 'We organised quite a few viewings but a lot of people found the prices were too high. They didn't want to pay that much for a 40-year lease. Another big bugbear was the fact you have to share toilets and you can't stay overnight.'

Clearly, there was demand elsewhere. When I was in Suffolk I had seen a poster advertising beach huts. *Want whole season beach hut hire from April to October?* it asked. *Then why not add your name to our waiting list!* Underneath someone had written, unequivocally, 'That's a joke!' A Waveney spokesman told local newspaper *The Journal* that in Lowestoft there were currently 144 beach hut sites and 194 seasonal lets, but this was failing to keep up with demand. The spokesman said, 'There are currently circa 500 names on the waiting list for beach huts – 130 for sites and 370 for huts. The average wait is 10 to 15 years for a site or hut to become available.'

Wayne Hemingway, it turned out, wasn't alone in appreciating the combination of architecture and the seaside. In Lincolnshire, there has been a Beautiful Beach Hut competition at Sutton on Sea since 2006, its aim being to utilise the beach huts, which have been much loved in the local area since the 1950s. The Beautiful Beach Hut competition is part of the wider Bathing Beauties Festival, 'the longest linear coastal arts festival in the world' (a more impressive accolade you could not imagine). The festival has music, poetry and fire, always a dangerous combination in my experience.

The Sutton on Sea beach huts were made of concrete, which I now know from talking to Wayne Hemingway was known in architectural circles as mid-century modern concrete. As well as the more eccentric designs, the beach huts to hire during your holidays are reasonably priced and more popular than ever.

The huts built as part of the competition were as exciting a discovery as anything I'd seen at any seaside. There is the beach hut for 'gazing and canoodling' designed by We Made That, an architecture and design studio: 'within an inconspicuous, black hideaway,' the studio described, 'the hut's indulgent interior with its Canoodling Bench invites hours spent in the company of an intimate companion.'

'The Cloud Bar', once a disused bus shelter on the beach at nearby Anderby Creek has been recognised by the Cloud Appreciation Society as the world's first 'Official Cloudspotting Area', and since its launch has been open to the cloudspotting public, who can stand on what looks like a wooden fort, poles high in the sky with adjustable mirrors to angle at the cloud of your choice. It looks like a low-budget Jodrell Bank, with boards explaining the kind of clouds you might be able to see.

Perhaps the best beach hut of all was 'Come Up and See Me', a huge replica gin and tonic, with a straw. This was designed by Michael Trainor, who conceived the whole Bathing Beauties idea. He is a professional artist who, like Hemingway, has long been associated with the seaside. An earlier project of his, *They Shoot Horses Don't They*, was responsible for producing what is believed to be the world's largest mirror ball on Blackpool seafront. 'Every second of every day,' Trainor explained on the BBC website, 'the mirrored facets give a different view of the environment – sea, sky, traffic, trams and promenades all wrapped up in one mesmerising, moving image.' This huge gin and tonic was just as impressive, though rather less romantically, inside, where you will find the official competition sponsors TL Risk Solutions.

Bathing Beauties was all about capturing something special about the coastline. It has been an extremely successful competition, commissioned by Lincolnshire County Council.

Yet you don't need a competition or an initiative or a festival to see art within beach huts. Whether in Southwold,

Scarborough or Bournemouth, just walking along the array of beach huts tells you all you need to know about the seaside. They're already like exhibitions, each one of them is like a three-minute pop song, every hut as evocative as a painting on display at the Turner Gallery.

It wasn't just for its beach pods that Boscombe was becoming known, but also its surf reef. The reef first opened in 2009. It cost around £1.4 million and was the only artificial surf reef in Europe, one of only four in the world.

Bournemouth Borough Council produced a fact sheet to explain how the reef would work. Its function was not to create waves, but to act 'as a ramp which changes the way the waves break and will certainly improve the quality of the surf'. The idea was that communities of surfers would arrive to enjoy the huge artificial waves, rejuvenating the local restaurants and hotels. Maybe they'd even hire a beach pod to use while they were in town. But, since a boat propellor damaged it in 2011, what had been intended to be the town's unique selling point had become just another example of a British seaside town council scratching its heads, trying to work out where it all went wrong and what would be the consequences. Judging by local newspaper reports and forums on surfing websites it was starting to seem likely that the reef would never be repaired, a real shame, not just for the area but for fans of surfing across Europe.

There had been a surprising number of surfers around the seasides I'd visited. A few months earlier I had stumbled upon a surf exhibition (probably called *Surf's Up!*, but I don't remember) at Coventry's Museum of Transport. In the entrance were Morris Minors, surfboards, VW camper vans and a quote from Formula 1's Damon Hill, now a keen surfer: 'If you have not slept in the car on the beach just to be the first to the surf you are not a surfer.'

I am not a surfer. I would love to be, but it will never happen; I don't have the rhythm or the grace or a surfboard. I wouldn't like all the falling in. But in this exhibition I started to realise I was clearly missing out on something. The film *Bikini Beach* played on loop, there were posters from adverts and magazines and across the room we were being taught the chronology of surfing. A beach buggy was on display, probably the coolest vehicle I've ever seen in my life.

'I loved the look,' its owner, Mark Knell, explained on the museum display. 'I think it was those big fat back tyres and the engine sticking out at the back and the way it looked like a toy and wanted to be played with.' Knell revealed the reason he owned the buggy in the first place. 'When I hit 40 I had a heart attack, and after that I thought "why not?" and bought a buggy. It is the only car that everyone, young or old will wave at you.'

Despite its strong associations with the West Coast of America, surfing's origins actually began with the British when Captain Cook's sailors arrived in Hawaii and Haiti. It wasn't until much later that surfing was seen at the British seaside. In 1959, Newquay introduced full-time lifeguards to their beaches and these lifeguards began to use surfboards to help with rescues.

At the same time, American and Australian surfers arrived in the UK and the sport really began to grow, as did the surfing community. Those early adopters of surf culture would strap their boards to the roof of their car and drive to the beach. As well as the boards being something to surf on, they were also the perfect indicators to other surfers. 'We are surfers!' they were saying to other motorists. If ever two cars with boards strapped to the top passed, they would pull over and get to know each other, excited at meeting like-minded people. 'We like surfing too!' they'd say, high -fiving. High-tenning, even, knowing what surfers are like. In the 1970s Morris Minor Travellers and VW camper vans became associated with the hippie movement. Surfers were quick to distance themselves from being hippies but they do share similar life views, mainly their willingness to distance themselves from the everyday.

Car enthusiasts are people I have always been baffled by. It's something that doesn't interest me at all. Jeremy Clarkson would hate me – something I'm not losing any sleep about. Surfing, by contrast, I understand. I get it. If I were a surfer I would spend hours waxing my board. It's living life slightly on the outskirts of society. As someone who was becoming increasingly obsessed with the seaside, it was a viewpoint I understood completely. These were people who embraced a different life, one of friendships, surfboards, living outside the norms.

Another example of the importance of surfing and making the most of living at the seaside is Freedom Surf, a disabled surfing project based at Fistral Beach in Newquay. Their mission is 'to provide fun and life-changing surfing experiences for people with physical disabilities, autism and special educational needs'. Freedom Surf has grown and developed into one of the leading disability surf schools in the UK. It was set up by Mark Hill and run as a not-for-profit organisation: 'I've taught soldiers who have had their legs blown off, people with cerebral palsy, those suffering from depression, as well as wayward youngsters, and the effect is almost always the same; the moment they get in the water, that fear and anger dissolves. It's like watching them wake up after a bad dream,' he explained to the charity Sports Leaders UK.

Freedom Surf has now worked with over 100 people with different disabilities, including cerebral palsy, muscular dystrophy, high- and low-functioning autism, Huntington's disease, MS, spina bifida, blindness and paraplegia. They've worked with children with special educational needs from schools across Cornwall. It's an incredibly powerful story, one of community, of selflessness and of optimism.

Over the previous few months, whenever I was too far away from a seaside, I'd become increasingly aware of how people constantly live their lives rushing around. I never thought I'd say this, but I preferred the idea of a multi-coloured VW van with a spare tyre on the back heading to the coast. Spending so much time at the seaside has really affected the way I see city life. The way I look at towns and the way people live. There are so many non-places inland. It seems a shame to live somewhere you can't be proud of.

Walking back along the promenade, away from the pods, I felt much more comfortable with the traditional Bournemouth beach huts. I passed a discarded pair of flip-flops. A lady with a tartan blanket on her knees was asleep, her book on her chest. I watched a little boy in yellow swimming trunks pulling a toy truck on a piece of string, a grey-haired man with his feet up on a spare deckchair reading a Spike Milligan book. A motorised scooter had a walking stick balanced against it. A young couple were taking advantage of being able to use cutlery; tipping the chips from chip shop wrappings onto their enamel patterned plates, knife and fork poised.

Every beach hut told a story. Two kids had set up a jewellery stand, attracting an interested browser. A family played a game that had clearly been continually evolving throughout their holiday. You are not allowed to worry about homework at the seaside. A man with a sunburnt bald head rinsed cups in a washing-up bowl with *Test Match Special* being broadcast, accompanied by a whistling kettle. I'm sure if I'd stayed there long enough I'd have heard the untwisting of a lid of a bottle of gin and ice cubes being dropped into glasses.

There were much worse places to spend an afternoon. It's easy to be cynical about the necessity of these buildings – whether huts or pods – but for so many they are part of your holiday. They are where you spend your free time.

What more valuable investment can you make? I couldn't help thinking about the luxury of being in a beach hut when it's raining, the feeling of smugness on hearing the drops bouncing off the wooden rooftop.

Despite its perceived failings, the Boscombe project was a fascinating one, which I hoped would ultimately succeed, improve the area and be replicated in other seaside resorts. Clearly, the people of Boscombe were proud of the area. People who live at the seaside generally are. I'd found I was much more likely to get a positive reaction from someone who lived at the seaside talking about their local area than a negative one.

In every seaside town I'd been to I had hoped to see evidence of creativity and something challenging so that the town would not be like a decommissioned factory, waiting to be detonated. I liked the seaside businesses and individuals who were fighting what can be heard every morning on the *Today* programme, about the recession and unemployment. I loved the fight that the people of Boscombe and Bournemouth were putting up, trying to be innovative. That's what I thought of as I walked back along the front, the effort at cultural regeneration. The pier, the beach pods, the surfing. I later found out that in California there was a surfing competition for dogs. Those Californians are always one step ahead.

CHAPTER FIFTEEN

What Do We Want? Pasties!

I'd never been to Cornwall. As part of my journey around the seaside resorts of the UK, I was able to take advantage of people I knew who had associations with the seaside. I'd ask people's advice on where I could go, anywhere I should visit, suggestions of where to spend an afternoon or a weekend.

I was particularly interested to talk to people who had grown up by the seaside. Cleethorpes was fairly close to where I grew up, but it wasn't within walking distance. I wanted to know what it would be like to have the seaside at your disposal as a teenager. I couldn't get my head around the opportunities that would represent; to me it seemed the sort of thing that only existed in films and soap operas.

My friend Molly grew up in Falmouth, and suggested I come and stay with her one weekend when she was down there visiting her mum and dad. Molly and I had been friends for years, had been housemates until recently, and I was looking forward to visiting both her and Cornwall.

The train journey there was possibly the longest I've ever been on. Even by the time you get to Plymouth you have to continue going south and west. Distracting me from Radio 4's *Desert Island Discs* archive and the *Guardian*'s football podcast was the breathtaking scenery.

'Sit on the left-hand side if you can,' Molly had suggested. 'That's where you get the best views.'

There is little more enjoyable in life than being on a train, in no great hurry, as the train track touches the coast and you bend around Britain.

Falmouth has as impressive a nautical history as any other town in the UK. In 1688 Falmouth was made the Royal Mail packet station; ships carried mail to every corner of the British Empire. For over 150 years the town was the only place where the mail came in and out of the country, in the packet ships. Nowadays you are reminded of its rich heritage: the local Wetherspoon's is called The Packet Station.

On my first morning there Molly took me to Flushing, a five-minute journey across the Penryn river. This was the route Molly travelled to get to primary school every day. We waited there for the boat so she could re-create the route.

'If I was late for school I'd have to find a nice old man to give me a lift on his rowing boat,' Molly told me on a misty Falmouth afternoon. 'There were eight of us who used to get to school by boat. We were the "boat guys", a weird gang who met on the harbour every morning. We had to hang around together for half an hour every day after school finished because the boat didn't arrive to collect us until half three. Everyone else in the school was really jealous of us. That's what I liked to assume, anyway.'

Molly told me that originally she went to a more conventionally accessible primary school but hated it. She constantly told her parents how unhappy she was there.

'It was horrible, I couldn't stand it. I'd see the boat going across the river to the other school and I'd wish I could just get on it and go to the nice school. I would literally wish it. Eventually my mum and dad let me change schools and it made me so happy. Even though I was young I realised things can't be so bad if you're in the same class at school as a girl called Boudicca.'

The boat's skipper, Peter, collected the £2 fare from each of his passengers. The boat was rickety, rocky, tiny, but to those children going across the river to school it must have been such an adventure. There was a couple sat opposite us, possibly also there to reminisce. The Flushing Ferry is a business that has been run by Peter and Janet Hudson since 2006. Prior to that, it was operated for 20 years by Mike Clynick, running people across the water and back. The importance of the service is much clearer once you take a look at a map of the area. To get around the coast by road would be a considerable journey, and then there is the problem of parking. This is a much easier method of transport, not to mention the added advantage that life is always more fun when a boat is involved. I found that out on the 1994 French exchange, somewhere on the English Channel between Portsmouth and Saint-Malo.

I opened up one of the pasties we'd bought at 'the best place to buy pasties in Cornwall', according to Molly's dad. There are many bakeries in Falmouth, all competing to come up with the most unique variation, playing around with the coveted concept of what a pasty can be. Fresh to go are fish-and-chip pasties, chicken tikka flavour and, perhaps worst sounding of all, chocolate and banana flavour. We ordered two normal pasties. That's the kind of people we are.

The definition of what makes a genuine Cornish Pasty is a seriously litigious area. There have been wars fought with less controversy. When George Osborne announced a rise in VAT on heated pasties sold in bakeries there were protests in Falmouth, hundreds took to the street, with their cries of 'What do we want? Pasties! How do we want them? Hot and tax free.'

Fifty or so miles to the east of Falmouth is Callington, a small town where the now ubiquitous Ginsters was founded in the 1960s, satisfying the hunger of people in petrol stations throughout the UK ever since. In the 60s the Ginsters family hit upon the idea of converting their egg-packing plant into a small bakery and started making pasties.

So what defines a proper pasty? Phil Ugalde, chairman of the Proper Cornish Food Company, explained in an interview with the BBC that 'an authentic Cornish pasty must have a distinctive "D" shape and be crimped, or folded into a rope-like pattern, on one side – never on top'. Ugalde, also representing the Cornish Pasty Association, explained that there must be a 'filling of "chunky" beef making up at least 12.5 per cent of the pasty, swede, potato, onion and a light seasoning – no artificial ingredients and it must go into the oven raw'. In 2011 the European Commission granted Cornish pasties the prestigious honour of 'Protected Geographical Indication' status. This means that although they can be sold and heated elsewhere, the pasty must have been prepared in Cornwall.

'This is really tasty!' I said, having bitten into the buttered crust of my pastry and into the chunky layers of steak. As the boat engine revved up Molly laughed, slightly embarrassed.

'I felt genuine pride when you said that,' she admitted.

The water was fairly calm as we crossed but nevertheless the ride still felt choppy. On days when the wind had some oomph in it there must have been a few unsettled stomachs on board over the years. Just a few minutes later, before we even had time to finish our food, Peter Hudson was tying the boat to a peg in Flushing. Molly, I and the other passengers dismounted and another small group of 'boat guys' gathered for a lift back to Falmouth.

Flushing is rather quaintly described on the ferry service's website as 'an impossibly pretty fishing village, with real fishermen'.

'This is where I used to come to have long thinks when I was a pretentious teenager,' Molly remembered as we looked out at the harbour, a mismatched jumble of boats ranging from the luxurious to battered-looking trawlers bobbing up and down on the water.

'This was your Lassiter's Lake?' I asked. I struggle to make sense of things unless I can connect them to *Neighbours* in some way. We walked into the village. A sign warned: *SLOW, swans crossing.*

'It can get pretty edgy around here,' said Molly, who'd moved to London after Cornwall, and lived in Cardiff after that, before settling down in Norwich. 'Once, someone said *shit*.'

On a brick wall outside a house was a plaque that read, *On this site, September 5th, 1782, nothing happened.* We walked on past Molly's old school. It was playtime; two children looked out longingly from the railings, but there was little action for them to observe. At this time of year the village, with just 670 residents, is deserted. Which is why we were slightly taken aback to see a decapitated mannequin with its tits out, sitting on a deckchair in the winter mist, just by the main road. We chose to get away from the road as quickly as we could, lest it followed us or appeared in recurring nightmares for the foreseeable future.

The lack of people in the out-of-season months is more than compensated for with so many boating events when it gets warmer, notably the regatta every July. This is when the tourists flock in their Panamas to combine boat-related activities with walks in a peaceful, tranquil environment. The Henri Lloyd Falmouth Week has developed into the largest regatta in the South West, with visitor numbers usually exceeding 100,000 during the week.

This was the opposite end of the year, though, and it was just me, Molly and the decapitated mannequin, which was still there, in the fog, possibly tiptoeing behind us.

'If you go over there you can see my house,' Molly told me, pointing up a hill, 'but I can't be bothered to show you.' With that we went into a pub, its walls covered with pictures of boats. We ordered a couple of pints of locally brewed ale from the barman, who seemed confused at the presence of customers, and had to put his guitar down, and temporarily stop singing covers of Johnny Cash songs to serve us our lunchtime beer.

I got the sense that people really made the most of living on the coast in Falmouth, certainly more than at the other seaside towns I had visited so far. In some of the other places I had been to, the sea had seemed almost incidental; something to show guests, like a good bookshop, a cathedral, or a café that sells nice cake. But in Falmouth and Penryn, locals really appreciated the water, and valued its proximity. As the barman tuned his guitar, we had our pints, finished off the contents of our paper bag of pasties, and Molly told me about growing up so close to the beach.

I had always been jealous of anyone who lived within walking distance of a beach. Were people aware that living near a beach is a pretty incredible childhood luxury?

'Yeah, I did appreciate it,' Molly said. 'Obviously a lot of the time it was just "This is where I live", but sometimes it did sink in that I was somewhere special, unique. We did lots of things that at the time seemed really normal but looking back I guess the seaside played a pretty significant contributing factor in my life, especially when I was a teenager. My friends and I used to come to the sea, look out at the waves and shout out our wishes. They were always the same. I'd wish to be a famous actress, Jasmine would wish for a nice boyfriend, Emma would wish for a camper van so she could travel the world. One day we brought two other girls from school with us and told them about our wishing game. They both wished to be thin and beautiful. We didn't go to the beach with them again.'

Molly didn't become an actress, other than 'pissing about with plays at university', but is now a writer, which is better. She writes plays, poems, stories. I asked her about the influence coastal towns have on the creative process.

'The trouble with doing art here is that people don't seem to be able to ignore the sea,' Molly told me, sipping her beer. 'Art that's about the sea tends to be a bit "driftwoody". My dad is a printmaker and makes visual art and he ignores the sea, but that's not true of many people who live in places like Cornwall. You can look at some of his work when we get back. I think it's ace.'

The idea that local artists can't ignore the sea is an interesting one. Many artists live by the sea because they have chosen to. There is something about the stillness of the water, the colours, the fresh air. Whenever you talk to someone about the seaside it is likely that art or creativity will be mentioned as a key factor in why they have chosen to live by the sea.

Molly's dad's art was, as Molly critiqued, ace. Molly and I had lived together for two years (not in the biblical sense), which meant I had seen samples of it already. She had his prints on the walls in her bedroom and I had told her then how much I liked them, before I even knew I was supposed to. Luckily it turned out they were by her dad, so she'd beamed a proud smile at my approval.

Despite her inability to draw even a convincing stick man, the rest of Molly's family are all artists: illustrators, painters, etchers. When I'd arrived at her house I'd seen three etched cityscapes on the mantelpiece in her front room.

'Which one of your lot did them?' I'd asked.

'Max,' she told me. Max is the elder of her two brothers, who both now live in London. 'Both of them apologised to my parents, they said they couldn't afford decent Christmas presents last year so they gave them paintings they'd made instead, as if that isn't the best possible thing in the world you can give.' The city skyscrapers in the etchings couldn't be further from the harbour Molly and I walked across, looking out at the boats, the sun setting behind Flushing.

The next morning, as the fishermen of Falmouth would have been casting their rods, Molly took me for a long walk to Pendennis Castle, one of two forts built by Henry VIII to guard the entrance to the River Fal. We went for a cream tea in Dolly's tea room, then we went to a pub where Molly beat me at pool.

I couldn't remember the last time I had felt so relaxed, and I think a big part of that was being in such close proximity to the water. It is somewhere I have always associated with being protected – there is something completely soothing, which is why I've loved spending time in so many coastal towns. I just looked forward to enjoying them again later in the year in a slightly warmer climate.

After the pub we went to the beach and sat on the sand, the night sky mysterious but protective all around us. The beach at night is so desolate. There's something eerie that happens to it at night.

I didn't tell Molly, but I am one of those people who knows that no matter what else happens in life, at a certain age I will move to the seaside, get a dog and a bungalow, and write a novel, or a play, or, God help us, buy an acoustic guitar. This possibility was becoming increasingly real to me now too, being worried about money and work and what I was doing with my life.

Whenever anything has been stressful in life, the seaside has been my happy place – somewhere I know I can run away to. I always figured I could learn to fish, make new friends, and eat nothing but seafood while working on sparkling prose. Whether or not my stories were ever published or read by anyone else was incidental, because that wasn't part of the plan: the only aims of my mission were to write and to be by the seaside.

If I could have painted, I would have been like the artists whose work appeared on the walls of every pub we'd been in. I'd have used an easel or a sketchbook and a row of sharp, coloured pencils to illustrate every grain of sand, every wisp of a cloud. Nothing in the world would have stopped me from painting trawlers, sunsets reflecting on the rippling surface of the water, a crowd in top hats and flowing frocks cheering at a regatta. My retirement destination of choice was always Whitby. Me and a Jack Russell.

'This is where Sally and I saw a ghost once,' Molly told me, as I thought about Whitby and my not-yet-born dog, and I realised how vivid your imagination gets when you're in darkness by the sea.

'Hey, we should go for a swim tomorrow,' Molly suggested. I said yes, because I assumed it was one of those ideas people have at 10pm that never actually happen. But the next morning there she was with her towel under her arm, ready to go. We were going swimming. In the cold, cold sea.

Local newspapers love the story of someone going for a swim on Christmas Day. Ideally it will be a pensioner. If they've received a letter from the Queen it could make front page of the local paper in the slow news period between Christmas and New Year. If they go swimming every day of the year, that's a double-page spread. On Christmas morning, members of Brighton Swimming Club – England's oldest swimming club, founded in 1860 – go for a morning dip in the sea. In 2011, there had been 30 swimmers as well as hundreds of spectators, including people dressed in fancy dress. For some people a Christmas swim in the sea is as much a tradition as watching the Queen's speech.

The health benefits of swimming in the sea have been talked about for years. Seawater contains amino acids, which help a healthy immune system. It opens pores in the skin to expel disease-causing toxins from the body. Swimming in the sea helps circulation and restores essential minerals depleted by stress caused by everyday life, poor diet and poisons from the environment. It activates the body's healing mechanism to fight asthma, arthritis, aches and pains, soothes skin and increases calmness. In the 18th century it was first claimed that cold water, and then seawater, were miracle cures. Sir John Floyer's *History of Cold Bathing* reached its fifth edition by 1722. Seawater was taken home in bottles to use therapeutically.

A swim in the sea sounded like exactly what I needed after a hectic few weeks. 'I came here one New Year's Day,' Molly told me, 'and people on the beach who were walking their dogs applauded me when I got out and ran to my towel!' Suddenly there was an incentive: the approval of strangers. The health benefits appealed to me as well. Life is stressful, and swimming has always been the one form of exercise I've been faithful to. Nothing can beat plunging into cold water on a hot day. Or even on a cold day.

'You have to make sure you mentally prepare yourself,' Molly warned. 'It will be so, so cold but all we have to do is complete one full stroke and we'll have done what we came for.'

Even so, I still wasn't fully prepared for what was about to happen.

'You're not going in, are you?' a lady asked, seemingly worried for us as we stood by the shore.

'Yep.'

'It will be freezing!' she exclaimed.

We might have been under-prepared and inexperienced, but we had worked out that the Falmouth sea would be a little on the cold side. It was too late for us to change our minds. Molly and I, stripped down to our swimming costumes, left a pile of clothes behind us, our worries and anxieties tucked up in the soles of our shoes with our watches and loose change. We counted '1, 2, 3 ...' and ran into the sea, doing our best approximation of breaststroking around while screaming in ice-cold agony. I had planned on putting my head underwater, but it was so cold I genuinely felt I'd die. We swam a little, shrieking as a coping mechanism, primal screaming all our fears and bank statements and bad backs and worries away. We were probably in the water for no more than a minute and a half before hurriedly swimming back to shore, grabbing our stuff and running to the toilets to get changed, taking comfort with the heat from the hand dryers.

'It's changed my life,' Molly said when we went for a walk afterwards, wet towels and costumes rolled up in our bags. We were both buzzing after the euphoria of the intense temperature change. 'I always feel so happy when I've been swimming in the sea. It makes me think more clearly, I feel more assertive, more creative. It's the endorphins. It's important to do things in life that scare you.'

I could feel the toxins already being released from my body. Admittedly, I didn't have any feeling in my feet; as a natural worrier I was fairly sure I wouldn't make it through the night, but when I managed to banish those feelings of imminent pneumonia I started to buzz at the experience of something at first dramatic and then soothing. It's one of the three times in my life I have felt genuinely alive, and the other two were both during the same episode of *The Bill*, so it was a pretty invigorating feeling.

'This is taking a really long time', Molly said as my tummy rumbled. It was the next day, and Molly and I had gone for breakfast in a café. We were in no rush, but after about half an hour we still had no food in front of us.

'I'm going to say something,' I said, uncharacteristically brave. I'm not one of those guys. I'd rather just stay hungry forever than have to deal with confrontation, but when the waitress walked past us I called her over and asked where the food was. She admitted she must have forgotten to put the order through. Molly asked how long it would be, and as politely and eruditely as we could we asked for the situation to be resolved. The duty manager came over, apologising, saying whatever we wanted we could have for free, that he was incredibly sorry and he was glad we had said something.

'That's because we went swimming in the sea,' Molly said as we went on our way, full of complimentary food and Appletiser. 'That kind of thing always happens when I've been for a swim in the sea. You feel good about yourself, do things you wouldn't otherwise have done, feel able to stick up for yourself, be assertive. Swimming in the sea gives you special powers. Neither of us would ever have done that normally. It's a good feeling, isn't it?'

I realised it was the first time ever I'd made a complaint in a restaurant, and it was all down to the previous day, swimming in the Falmouth sea. If I hadn't been to stay with Molly for those few days there was no way I would ever have considered jumping in. But the feeling I had afterwards had completely changed my outlook, I felt so refreshed and re-energised, that I had a healthy body and a healthy mind. The people in the 18th century had been right all along.

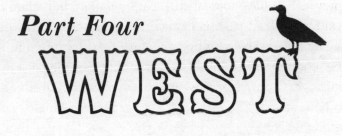

Part Four

WEST

CHAPTER SIXTEEN

A Bucket and Spade Extravaganza

Despite terrible storms all across the UK on a day in July, one corner of the weather map was spared a rain cloud. Luckily it was Woolacombe in North Devon, the venue of the UK National Sandcastle Competition, although admittedly it was more woolly hat than sombrero weather.

I'd been pretty worried about the weather, knowing there was a chance that the rain would almost certainly ruin everyone's fun, not to mention limit the money they were raising for charity. There's something about a windy, rainy seaside town that many find enchanting and special, but this was a sandcastle competition. We weren't asking for much, just minimal drizzle.

Out on the beach, the rain clouds were dispersing and the sun was thinking about breaking through. A little boy in yellow swimming trunks wrote 'Calvin' on the sand with a big stick. A family organised a game of rounders. Mum and dad were arguing. One of the boys was taken to one side while his dad had a 'Don't ruin this for everyone' word with him.

'Once you're out you have to field,' the dad explained. I have never liked that rule.

Beach rounders is a little like Monopoly. No two games are exactly the same. If you go round to someone's house and play Monopoly, it is likely there is a variation from your own version of the game, to do with Free Parking, or the stations, or what happens if someone doesn't want to buy a property. This is the same with beach rounders. It has been adapted by each family, year on year, at a variety of beaches across the country, the world even.

A girl bowled underarm and a little boy hit the ball, not hard, and he only ran to first base. There was no-one fielding on first base. That's bad captaincy. It's a vital position. The next batter hit the ball, ran to first base, second base, but then went too far, didn't make third base and he was out. He took it incredibly well, and took a place out fielding for the other team, who moments ago had been his sworn enemies. Next in to bat was the dad, and he leathered it. 'Rounder! Rounder! Rounder!' they all chanted. On its completion he picked up the little boy and they celebrated together. 'Well done, Daddy,' said the little girl bowling. I stopped watching. This family harmony could not last. Soon there would be arguments.

The sandcastle competition wasn't due to start for a couple of hours but already two ten-year-olds were building a sandcastle next to me. It was the best sandcastle I'd ever seen in real life, complete with two Union Flags flying majestically, worthy of a visit from a minor member of the Royal Family.

For me, making the perfect sandcastle was always the same as flying a kite and making a big cake, it's something I'd always wanted to do, but whenever I've tried, I've failed. Some things are just beyond me; the reality was so different to the picture in my mind that it was devastating so, as with most things, I just stopped trying. A sensible approach in the long run.

Especially as building sandcastles is becoming an increasingly competitive pastime. Every year, around 8,000 people take part in the UK National Sandcastle Competition on Woolacombe Beach. On the train down to Woolacombe, I had looked at the competition's website. Photographs of past entries included sand tortoises, shells, a hippo, Shaun the Sheep, dragons and igloos. I had no idea it was possible to be so creative with just sand.

I spoke to Rebecca, one of the organisers of the competition. She explained that the original idea came from a local construction company. To start with it had been a corporate team-building event, but it had loosened up over the years, and now anyone is allowed to take part. Some people plan in advance, arriving with drawn-out designs and step-by-step instructions, whereas other people just turn up.

Sometimes spontaneity is the best policy. The people who were runners-up the previous year had arrived on the day without realising a competition was taking place. They'd joined in, building a fire-breathing dragon, proof that you don't have to be a graphic designer or work in construction to take part. Their success encapsulated the idea that the sandcastle-building competition was for everyone – an opportunity to be creative for the day, whether you're a young family or a group of solicitors who work together. It's all about having fun; there's a samba band, a live DJ. The competition has now become a fixture in people's diaries so they know to come down and watch, bring a picnic, a camera, and hang out with friends.

Rebecca and her colleagues were a team of six who organised the event to raise money for the North Devon Hospice, which provides care and support to patients diagnosed with a life-limiting illness, as well as providing support for those who love them. Organising the sandcastle competition was an opportunity for people to come together: much-needed money is raised by the teams' entry fees, corporate sponsorship, and bucket collections on the day. Perhaps it is revealing that the second-placed team in the competition were not families or groups of children, but a golf club.

Locally and nationally, the event gets lots of coverage. Last year Heart FM presented from there. The previous year Children's BBC had come along to film. *Countryfile* had been there too, and Paddy McGuinness and Rory McGrath came one year to film for another TV show. Paddy was on one team, Rory on the other; an embargo in place so they couldn't advertise their attendance in advance. Or perhaps because otherwise people wouldn't have turned up. 'Oh God, not those two blokes off the telly.'

It wasn't just Rebecca, solicitors on their day off, or Rory and Paddy who were passionate about sandcastles. English Heritage had started to worry that 'in the techno-savvy 21st century it may be in danger of becoming a lost art' and so launched a nationwide Ultimate Sandcastle Competition. This wasn't an intense day of scrabbling around with work colleagues, friends and video cameras, but was to be carried out in your own free time. The specific brief was for people to build sandcastles based on a castle within the care of English Heritage and post a picture of it on the organisation's Facebook page. English Heritage exists 'to make sure the best of the past is kept to enrich our lives today and in the future': sandcastles seem to be as important a part of our heritage as anything. When I spent time with Gerry the retired lighthouse keeper, he told me he used to get sent paintings of lighthouses made as part of school projects. He was proud of the fact that if you ask any child to draw a picture of the seaside there will be a lighthouse standing tall on the coast with its red and white stripes. In the foreground will be sandcastles with battlements, flags, a little moat.

In Lyme Regis, meanwhile, there is a sandcastle and sand sculpture competition as part of the annual Lifeboat Week: a fundraising event that also includes gospel choirs, a Red Arrows display, art exhibitions, a meet and greet with local lifeguards and a bathtub race. Another competition was held in Burnham-on-Sea in Somerset, where 993 sandcastles were built in an hour, beating the world record. Three independent adjudicators had measured every castle, with it taking about six weeks to verify the record with Guinness World Records. There were very specific instructions: the sandcastles had to be two feet high, two feet across and have four turrets.

'More than a hundred were disqualified but we still managed to smash the record,' organiser Steve Bird told BBC Somerset.

So what's the secret behind making a good sandcastle? The key component, according to experienced sandcastle builders, is moist sand. A key piece of advice I found from an internet message board was to add the sand to water, rather than the other way round: 'get a large bucket of water, and add sand by the handful or by the shovel scoop until you've got a soppy mess of sand that just barely holds together when you grab a handful out of the bucket and squeeze it. The sand should be solid enough to keep some shape, but wet enough to be easily manipulated.'

The next thing to do is build a mound of this wet, sloppy sand. Pat it, mould it into the shape you want it to be, whether it's a castle, a ship, or a sexy mermaid. Chip away at it, like a sculptor with a block of marble. Sandcastle-building experts and pro sandcastle builders call this technique the 'softpack', because you start with a soft pile and then pack it with your hands until it is hard and firm. To help you with this you can bring special equipment. Tool up; using a paintbrush, pastry knife, toothpick or lolly stick can help with trims and decorations.

Using lots of water is crucial because dry sand does not want to stand up or be shaped; it wants to lie down. The best sand sculptors do not use buckets, but instead build the shape of their sandcastles by stacking handfuls of wet sand. There are even more extreme methods suggested. One intense theory I found when fulfilling my vital role of Googling sandcastles is that you need 'clean, dry sand; sodium silicate; water; a pair of rubber gloves; a thin rubber tube; sand moulds and buckets; a mixing tray; a carbonating tray; a large clear plastic bag; carbon dioxide from a SodaStream machine'. It was a tactic that involved building your sandcastle at home and taking it along to the beach with you. I wasn't entirely sure that was entering the spirit of the British seaside, tapping a bucket with a soon-to-break spade, hoping it wouldn't crumble with the final reveal. But this level of competitiveness is nothing new. Sandcastles have been treated as a serious pastime for generations. What I thought was just something to occupy toddlers for an afternoon is actually something incredibly complex.

Sand sculpting's origins are just after the First World War, when it wasn't so much about aesthetics or competition, but about making money. These sculptors were not just artists but entrepreneurs, finding an innovative way to make money on the beach. They were often friends with the Punch and Judy puppeteers and the ice cream vendors – all offering entertainment to packed beaches under the watchful eye of the beach inspector, who was also there to observe dress codes.

One fascinating sand sculptor of recent years is a man from Yorkshire called Baldrick Buckle, who co-founded the company Sandaholics Anonymous in 1997. The company was hugely successful around the world, and created the largest sand sculpture ever built in the Middle East. But Buckle grew tired of it all, quitting Sandaholics in 2002, describing sand sculpture on the Sandworld website as '… too much Mickey Mouse and not enough Salvador Dali', and left to work with the Iraq football team. Buckle described this part of his life as '… the point when I realised life's possibilities, it is truly possible to shape your life into anything that you choose … and re-shape'.

The man widely credited as being the first sand sculptor was Fred Darrington, who created sand sculptures on Weymouth Beach from the 1920s. After his death in 2002 he was described in his *New York Times* obituary as being to British sandcastles 'what Sir Christopher Wren was to London churches'. When the tide went out he would make huge sandcastles for the public to admire. They would throw coins into the castles to show their appreciation. Darrington was self-taught and became one of the world's acknowledged masters of sand sculpting. His grandson Mark helped him out from the age of 11. Mark would fetch his granddad cups of tea and learn how to mix the sand. He became an apprentice in 1988 but his granddad never told him what to do; but, as is revealed on the Sculptures in Sand website: 'Mark knew he had succeeded when he turned up for work one day to find Fred had changed the sign to "Sand Sculptures by FG Darrington & Grandson".'

Mark ended up running the company that his grandfather had started. He was commissioned to create a sandcastle on Weymouth Beach as part of the build-up to the London 2012 Olympic Games. It took him four full days to create, and when finished it was 13 feet high, complete with Union Flags and Olympic rings. But, according to a *Daily Telegraph* article, 'the structure was knocked down shortly after it was finished, due to concerns about health and safety'. Soon after the departure of the photographers, 'the castle was destroyed by a mechanical digger', squashing the hours and hours of meticulous crafting to create something that from the photographs was a pretty incredible sight.

Simon Williams, head of the Weymouth and Portland 2012 Operations Team, said, 'It was an organisational decision. We took it down because it was constructed in a special way and we couldn't have just left it there in case it fell on a young child.' Some people questioned the logic of spending £5,000 on a structure that would be around for minutes.

For some seaside towns, though, even building a simple sandcastle is more complicated than you would imagine. Lyme Regis, because of erosion, resorted to importing 30,000 tonnes of sand from Normandy for one of its four beaches. Nick Browning, the project manager for importing sand as well as pebbles and shingle, told the BBC: 'We needed a grain of a certain particle size to stop it from being washed away. It also has to be the right colour.'

Paradoxically, at the same time that the Weymouth Olympic sandcastle was being knocked down, Greenwich Beach, 'London's first long-term beach', was set to open near the O2 Arena, with an Olympic-size volleyball court and plans for a restaurant and live events stage, which was set to be open to the public every June to September until 2017. Managing director of the project, Frank Dekker, explained that 'children and young people in the city will have an opportunity to get the sand between their own toes. The Olympic-standard beach volleyball court will offer young people the opportunity to exercise in an interesting and novel way.' This is Greenwich they were talking about, 40 miles from Southend-on-Sea. What happened to going out on a day trip? There seems something incredibly unnecessary about an artificial beach. Nothing seems straightforward in the 21st century. Not even building a sandcastle.

With the sandcastle competition finally under way under cloudy skies, it made me realise how little we need the sunshine. We just need it to be all right. You can have fun at the beach with your jacket on. Obviously being on the beach in 30-degree heat is a special experience, but you can't have it all the time.

They didn't have that when my grandparents were young. They didn't need the sunshine. It was about escapism, getting away. My mum in Redcar never needed the sunshine. The Beacocks didn't need the sunshine for Beacock family cricket. None of us need the sunshine. If it's there we enjoy it. We can, though, prepare ourselves if it's going to be a bit damp and drizzly. We just have to take the right attitude with us to the seaside. It might rain but we'll be all right.

That fighting spirit is increasingly rare. The dogs don't care if it's sunny, so why should we? We don't need the sunshine. We just like it to be dry. Not too windy. I've enjoyed being at the seaside in all conditions. The boating lake doesn't need the sunshine. The crazy golf players don't need the sunshine. And neither did those in the sandcastle building competition.

CHAPTER SEVENTEEN

My Very Own Marco's Mug

'Cantona got married in a lighthouse!' Molly had shouted excitedly in Falmouth, when I was updating her with my stories about my travels. Of all the people I had met, it had been Gerry the retired lighthouse keeper she had been particularly keen to hear about. 'Cantona' was our friend Lisa, who once dressed up as Eric Cantona for a fancy dress party; the Manchester United number 7 shirt and the football she glued to her foot earned her what we hoped would be a nickname for a lifetime.

Lisa now lived in Cardiff, and I met up with her on the next leg of my seaside journey: South Wales. She told me all about her wedding at Nash Point Lighthouse, one of the increasing number of lighthouses offering marriage ceremonies.

'We were shown around by Gerald, one of the caretakers of the lighthouse,' Lisa/Cantona explained. 'He was incredible. When we got to the room on the fourth floor, he told us people got married there. We looked at each other and that was that. It was decided.'

Lisa, easily my favourite Welsh person, told me they left the lighthouse and went to the snack cabin nearby and had tea (in mugs) and Welsh cakes and sat on the top of the cliff and for the first time talked about their wedding. It all seemed so right. 'Why it was so certain, I don't know,' Lisa continued. 'Maybe it was because it was a bit silly. Or because it felt like no matter what else happened, no matter if our families got on or didn't, or if the food was disappointing later on, or if it shitted rain down, it would be a little magical thing that happened in the tiniest of round rooms on the edge of a Welsh cliff.'

I was disappointed I hadn't been friends with Lisa and her husband John at the time. I'd have loved an invitation to a lighthouse wedding. She told me about the big day, all concrete and cold: 'I walked down the stairs holding hands with my dad, to the music of Jon Hopkins. I had a lump in the throat. And on the way down he kicked a glass candleholder through the bars and it smashed into tiny pieces. And that was good because it got rid of the lump and made me laugh.'

Lisa now works as a digital storytelling producer, something she's been able to apply to her experience with the lighthouse: 'After I got married there I had all this emotion wrapped up in the lighthouse, but didn't really know what to do with it. I didn't know anything about the place itself and I just kept going back time and time again and walking about. So I decided to record the people who had a relationship to the place.'

Lisa explained how she'd spoken to the caretaker who'd been there on her wedding day: 'I found out he'd been the keeper at Nash Point when he was 18, 30 years earlier. He'd hated it. He was lonely and wanting to drink in a pub and go for chips and kiss girls. And he couldn't. He was in a lighthouse. He left two years later and said he'd never ever go back. He became a businessman and made himself a bit ill with stress and life. And then he saw a job advert, at Nash Point Lighthouse. He loves it now. He's the happiest he's ever been.'

Lisa's audio theatre piece allowed people walking around Nash Point to listen to the stories of the people who care about it. She spoke to the people who run the cabin who served them the tea in mugs and Welsh cakes that day. Her story of marrying John was in there too. The stories of people who loved that lighthouse. All these seaside buildings have voices and memories reverberating within their walls, but Lisa had snatched voices from the ether, transferred them to a USB stick.

Lisa suggested I should talk to her friend Carl Chapple, an artist who lived nearby in Cadoxton, a small village a few miles from Barry Island. I'd already been planning on visiting Barry Island, so this was perfect. When I spoke to Carl on the phone, he said he would be more than happy to meet me: 'My house is just opposite the park,' he explained, a nice detail to be able to drop into a set of directions.

When I met up with Carl, he was keen to show me some train advertisement posters from the 1950s, which he'd found on his computer the day before. His favourite was for Barry Island, a slogan possibly not quite as overwhelming as had been intended: *Go to Barry, for varied enjoyment.* These were the days before PR, before people could study subjects like advertising and brand management at university. 'Experts' today would probably say you've got to be slightly more upbeat in your promotional material. I disagree. The poster made me want to go to Barry Island all the more.

We took our mugs of tea up to his studio on the top floor of his house. Carl, wearing a Josie Long T-shirt, showed me portraits he had painted in London, all of them postcard size. 'Being here with so much space has meant I have been able to expand and improve and try out new things. Light and space are crucial. Moving to the seaside really liberated my work, it meant I could move away from the analytical style of oil sketches onto canvas and be more spontaneous.'

I asked him how close we were to the sea.

'It's just over there!' he said, pointing out of the window. A trampoline placed at the correct angle and you'd just need to take a run and jump and you'd land on the sand. 'I've lived here for nine years and recently found a brand new deserted beach I'd never been to before. I didn't even know it existed. I go running there every morning now. That's what it's like round here. Always discovering new places.'

Carl specialised in portraits, which were pegged across the room; a canvas in the centre of the studio was a self-portrait, a bearded man looking jolly, possibly because he lived so close to the seaside. Being in an artist's studio was so much more exciting than being in a writer's office. I think many writers feel envious towards painters in the same way that stand-up comedians do towards film stars, the same ambition and frustrations that *Home and Away* actors feel about being pop singers. I was buzzing with excitement just looking around the studio; there were pots full of paintbrushes, palettes, spattered rugs on the floor, a digital radio almost certainly tuned into BBC Radio 6 Music, oils, blank canvases, row after row of paintings and prints.

'I lived in London before this,' Carl told me. He studied painting at St Martin's School of Art in London. 'Having grown up in South Devon where you can see for miles and miles, I never adjusted to the fact that no matter where you are in London you can't see for more than a quarter of a mile. It was strange. I was used to distant horizons.'

It was a clear day on my visit and Carl pointed out Weston-super-Mare, visible across the Bristol Channel. 'I started to think about moving away from London, I had been there long enough, then a job came up here in South Wales and it just seemed the perfect move to make. For a long time in London I had been frustrated about being so closed in. This was my opportunity to spread out.' Carl continued to explain how he had moved to the seaside to escape London. I'd found the theme of escape to be a recurring one at the seaside. Whether it was from a job, from a city or something existential, with every person I had met at the seaside, the word escape was never too far behind.

I'd been looking around the studio while Carl was talking, taking everything in: the studio, the seaside, the nice cup of tea. I noticed there didn't seem to be any paintings of beaches. I scanned the work on the walls of his studio but hadn't spotted any sea or sand, not even a painted sun with a smiley face on it.

'It's not really what interests me,' Carl said. 'I took my paints down to the beach once but I just ended up doing a shitty painting. A nine- or ten-year-old girl was watching me as I was working on it, in the way little girls do, and she just shook her head and walked off, moving sagely on. That told me quite a lot. I have painted landscapes and enjoyed it; I've spent days observing deer and that kind of thing. I came up with a couple of pictures I really liked, but it would have taken me 20 or 30 years to get good at it. It made sense to carry on with the portrait work. Painting landscapes doesn't interest me nearly as much as painting people.'

Carl was articulating exactly how I felt about spending so much time at the seaside. I was less interested in the landscape, I had been to places like Southwold, Brighton, Redcar. But what really fascinated me was not so much the architecture, the pebbles and the charcoal skies, but the couples who owned the B&Bs, the people who worked in the chip shops or were on the beach with metal detectors at 5am.

'With portraits, my concerns are about gesture and line and colour and trying to reveal something of the sitter,' Carl continued, 'as well as making it look at least approximately like them. With landscape painting it is so much more about depth and colour and perspective. These are things which don't come into my portrait painting very much. Trying to get into that headspace is very difficult. Beaches and coastal paintings don't excite me. I like to concentrate on specifics.'

As Carl showed me examples of his work, it was easy to tell which he had painted in London and which were produced in that studio by the beach he ran along every morning. That freedom and expression was tangible in every detail. This is the reason Lisa had been so keen for me to meet Carl. In order to grasp the importance of the seaside, what Carl was telling me was as vital as anything I'd been told by Mrs Martin at Brighton Pier, Chris in Skegness or Gerry with his lighthouses.

Although Carl wasn't particularly keen to paint the coast, I had come across a book by someone who clearly thrived on doing so. David Bellamy's book *The Wild Coast of Britain* is surely the most beautiful collection of paintings and sketches that has ever existed, certainly relating to the British seaside. Maybe that's too bold a claim, considering it's the only one I've ever looked at. I wanted to cut out every picture and stick them to the walls in my bedroom, but that would have ruined it for whoever borrowed it next from the library. The book has page after page of the exquisite and the simple, as well as Bellamy's own thoughts and experience of the British coast. He recalls the time he was trying to sketch Robin Hood's Bay but a dog wouldn't stop licking his face, an image that is worth the price of the book alone, or certainly the cost of the imminent overdue fine.

Bellamy was an artist, botanist, broadcaster and owner of one of the most cherished voices for generations, whether it was for his television programme *Bellamy's Britain*, his countless appearances on programmes such as *Blue Peter*, or providing the voiceover for Ribena adverts. He produced several books from the coastlines of Great Britain. On his 1978 appearance on *Desert Island Discs*, he told presenter Roy Plomley that his first job after leaving school was collecting deckchairs on Brighton beach. 'I used to cycle down and live under the Palace Pier where you could sleep for nothing, then work for the weekend, and having collected all the deckchairs on the Sunday I'd go back home again.'

His drawings are as relaxing and peaceful as going on holiday, perhaps even more so because they don't involve having to do any packing or unpacking. One recurring theme in his work is how fiercely concerned he is about the environment and the protection of our planet. *The David Bellamy Awards Programme* is a competition designed to encourage schools to be aware of, and act positively towards, environmental cleanliness. 'I would like to write about a beautiful coast,' he wrote in this book, 'unadulterated by the effluence of modern Britain, but sadly those in authority do not seem to care much for the state of our environment.'

In more recent years Bellamy has been vocal in his hatred of wind turbines, writing angrily on his own website about the building of wind turbines across Wales. He shows one of his own watercolours of Mid-Wales scenery, saying that before long this will be 'an artistic no-go area'. Personally I think there is something quite reassuring about the rhythms of the turbines, they add an extra dimension to landscapes and coasts.

For David Bellamy, as for Carl, the relationship between art and the seaside was something special. They weren't the only ones – Turner and Tracey Emin had felt something similar in relation to Margate and the Kent coastline. In fact, the more I learned about art at the seaside, the more I realised how it touched every corner of the British coastline.

One of the four major Tate galleries can be found in St Ives, overlooking the Cornish resort of Porthmeor Beach. In the six months after it was first opened in June 1993, the gallery focused on artists who had lived or worked in St Ives. One of the area's most celebrated artists was a local fisherman, Alfred Wallis. He began painting when he was well into his seventies, for company because his wife had died. His great-great-great nephew Andy Blair wrote about him, exhaustingly but poetically, saying that the works 'capture the smells and flavours of the sea; his colours replicating the candy coated light synonymous with the Penwith coastline and exposing us to the fragility of little men in flat caps hauling their catch to harbour against the turbulence of ferocious and unpredictable waters. And all this with a beauty so simplistic as to match the unspeakable effect of St Ives on those who have been there.'

Further north, on the Wirral peninsula, is New Brighton, a town associated with art largely because of work by the photographer Martin Parr. Parr is a self-proclaimed aficionado of the British seaside and his 1985 book *The Last Resort: Photographs of New Brighton* is 'a document of working-class vacationers', in which Parr captured and documented people on their holiday at the run-down resort. My favourite of his photographs is in his book *Think of England*, a zoomed-in shot of a man holding a cup and saucer, resting a fairy cake on his knee. Some of Parr's photographs have attracted controversy and he has been accused of snobbery and looking down on these people, particularly those of New Brighton. But for so many, the photographs encapsulate something so personal, images so easy to relate to. Parr is one of those artists about whom the word 'quintessential' will always be found in a press release or review. His photographs are like Kinks songs: he manages to create something that is everyday and to many would be barely noticeable but, once observed and photographed, will stay with you for a long time.

Just along from New Brighton is Crosby, home to another famous piece of seaside art: Antony Gormley's display of statues on the beach, an exhibition called *Another Place*. Gormley is most famous as the designer of the *Angel of the North* in Gateshead, the largest public statue in the country, though in their own way the beach statues are every bit as iconic.

I'd been fortunate enough to see the statues for myself on a previous visit to the area. *Another Place* consists of 100 cast-iron, life-size figures spread out along 3 kilometres. They're not just on the beach, either: the tide was in when I was there so I had to take off my shoes, roll up my trouser legs and wade in just so I could get up close. There had been a lot of local resistance towards the statues. Some concerns were about safety, that people may simply bump into the statutes, but another cause of concern was that Gormley had included the penises on the statues. Men, though, do have penises. Ask any scientist or doctor and they'll be able to tell you without having to look it up in a book. Gormley probably has one so why shouldn't his statues, which were made from casts of his own body? It wouldn't have looked right if they'd been wearing pants. If it was good enough for Michelangelo, it was fine for statues on Crosby beach.

Another Place was originally intended to be a temporary installation, from July 2005 until November 2006. Its popularity was such that years later they are still there, hence my being able to get my trousers wet, put my arm round a statue and take a photograph of myself with one of the fellas. Being so close to a statue was surprisingly moving, looking at the way he (and it is a he) was just standing there, liberated, exposed to the elements, staring out at the horizon. I looked out in the same direction, the two of us, practically arm in arm on a Thursday afternoon, the waves hitting the bottoms of our bare legs.

At times like this it was difficult not to start being contemplative. In 1995, Gormley created an exhibition called *Critical Mass*: 60 life-size cast iron body forms that went on display on the roof of the De La Warr Pavilion at the seaside resort of Bexhill-on-Sea in Sussex. Gormley's words when asked about that exhibition were just as relevant to where I was standing in Crosby. 'I am excited to see these dark forms in the elements against the sea and in direct light,' he'd said. 'It will be like a sky burial. How these masses act in space is very important. The challenge is to make the distance intimate, internal.' From my own visit to Crosby, I remember thinking there was such serenity with the Gormley statues. Each person who goes to see them will experience something unique and thought provoking, whether they are making a journey with the sole intention of looking at them or stumbling across them on the beach, thinking: 'What are these weird statues with their cocks out?'

Beaches are not static. At any moment in time the lighting will be different, the tide might be in or out, the sun setting, rising, hiding behind clouds. The beach might be crowded or deserted. Life offers so many interpretations; if I'd gone the next day or the next month, it would have been different in some way. When I visited, it was just me and the statues, facing out, anonymous faces with our backs to the world. We'd stood together, us lads, content at the seaside.

Back in South Wales, I'd taken the 15-minute journey from Carl's studio to one of the most unusual seaside resorts in the UK: Barry Island. If you can't manage regeneration schemes or heavy investment, just hope a hit BBC sitcom films at your seaside. Barry Island has benefited as much from *Gavin and Stacey* being filmed there as Brighton has from its pier. I now drink my tea out of a Marco's mug, sold by Marco, who runs the real-life café where the fictional Stacey worked. I felt embarrassed to ask for it but it was clearly something he was used to: he had hundreds of them stacked up to be flogged at decent profit to idiots like me. But I was genuinely excited to be on Barry Island. I was hoping James Corden or Ruth Jones might be around filming a documentary, reminiscing.

Barry was an odd place. There were Christmas decorations for sale in a shop by the beach, on the shelves either far too early, far too late or simply forgotten about. A little further along from the beach was the 'adiZone' – 'your space to experience sport and fitness for free'. No membership, just have a go at whatever took your fancy: cross trainers, treadmill, bikes, spongy tarmac. No need to put down jumpers for goalposts here. They use goalposts for goalposts. Two boys, too short for a slam-dunk, played basketball.

On the beach a man in a wetsuit carried a surfboard on his shoulder. I think it was one of the Beach Boys. A couple walked a dog. After so many seaside resorts, I still wasn't getting bored with them, the novelty still hadn't worn off. This was where I liked to be. I loved the idea of Carl's life, living so close to these beaches. It was a common feeling whenever I went to a seaside. The knowledge that I would be very happy there, a different pace of life.

CHAPTER EIGHTEEN

Dad's Pillbox

My dad grew up in Manchester in the 1950s. When he went on holiday it would be to North Wales, as was common for people from the North West. He would go with his mother, her sisters and their husbands, a ten-strong family group walking along the seafront. My grandma was a single mother and he was an only child, living in a terraced house full of aunties and linoleum.

'We only ever went on holiday in the summer,' he told me, sitting in his new conservatory, the building of which had occupied most phone conversations we'd had over the previous six months. I had come back to see him because we were going to Wales to visit places he remembered from holidays when he was younger. He explained how there was no money or time for a winter holiday, but during the last week in July and first week of August they always headed by train to Talacre, near

Prestatyn, or sometimes down the coast to Abergele in North Wales.

'Our holidays always began with a trip to the police station,' he continued. 'We always used to tell the police before we went away, the idea being that while the house was empty, the Manchester Police, having nothing better to do, should send the local bobby round every so often and check that the front door was still locked and that we hadn't been burgled. This went on for several years until the police pointed out that having a policeman go round rather advertised that we were away,' my dad laughed at the ludicrous process.

My dad remembered a day trip when they'd gone to Blackpool. He was walking alongside my grandma after she left a shop, but when he looked up to ask her something he realised it wasn't her. He'd been walking alongside a total stranger and suddenly realised he was completely disorientated and on his own. He wandered up and down the promenade until he was asked if he was okay by a policeman and taken to the lost children's section. He had to sit on a chair in a hut with nothing to play with, just watching other children playing with their families on the beach. Alongside him were other children in the same predicament. My dad remembered the hut being completely silent. No-one spoke to each other. They were just sat there in their own worlds waiting to be collected.

'Even now, 50 years later,' my dad said, 'I can still feel that relief of reconciliation when she poked her head round the door and we saw each other. I couldn't stop crying, and then was angry because she went off without me. I was so ungrateful! But I guess all kids that age are. The ingratitude of children!'

Another story was a time he had a donkey ride, again in Blackpool. He got up on the donkey but the attendant had to go to a shop to get some change. When the attendant got back he found the donkey running off into the distance, with my dad on its back and my grandma running after them.

I'd never really talked to my dad about his family holidays. I always knew they went away and I'd seen photos he'd shown me and my sister when we were younger: slides projected onto the living room wall until the day smoke started coming out of the projector and it had to be thrown in the dustbin, being held at arm's length by an oven glove. This presented a good opportunity to talk to him about his holidays growing up and, by proxy, the most vivid memories of his childhood. But it didn't seem enough to just hear his stories. I wanted to see these places for myself, and as I had the time and was exploring the British seaside, I asked if he'd like to go back, have a look, take me with him, let me make a mix CD for the journey.

'I've got some vague memories about my first holiday,' my dad told me, happy to talk about his childhood as we maintained a steady 70 on the M62. We were heading to Abergele. I'd heard him mention it there before, occasionally seen its name on the news or heard it on the Radio 5 Live travel, and thought it sounded like it would be a nice place, so had always wanted to go there to visit. I'm not much of a dreamer.

Their accommodation back in the late 1950s consisted of old railway carriages that were converted into residential caravans near the beach. Nowadays that would be the ultimate hipster accommodation frequented by people who work in the arts, but back then they had corrugated iron roofs that drummed with rain during the freezing cold nights and there was no running water. An early family photograph is of one of my dad's aunties carrying a bucket of water from the communal tap to the caravan for cooking and washing.

I'd never been to North Wales before. There was a magical quality about the names of the seaside places we were going to, the signposts we had driven past: Colwyn Bay, Llandudno, Abergele. There's something special about the arrangement of the letters in those words. They sound like the kind of seaside towns you want to visit rather than just hear stories about. When we arrived my dad pointed out a little boy in the car park wearing bright red wellies.

'I was that old when I was first here,' he said.

It was odd to think of my dad being a toddler.

'We came here because it was cheap,' my dad continued as we walked through Abergele. 'It was good because not only was it cheap, but there was nowhere to spend money.'

The first thing we did was head to the beach. With many seaside towns you feel like you are on the edge of something, but that was never the case more than with Abergele, where it is easy to feel you've been deserted, cut adrift from the rest of the world. A bingo game was being played in the amusement arcade. Three men and a lady sat to the tunes of 'clickety click's. Outside, the main attraction was a puddle in the car park. A whole family played in it in their wellies. They'd come prepared, splashing around. It was pretty deep. A good puddle.

'This is where we spent our holidays,' my dad said. He seemed proud. The places we go on holiday when we're growing up are such a big part of our lives. Showing someone around the place you regularly went to on holiday is almost as personal as showing your own home or early home movies, a shaky camera documenting first steps and rides on swings. It didn't take long before he found the 'flatlet' he used to stay in. Flatlets were different to conventional bed and breakfasts because although they were still run by strict landladies they catered for just one family at a time.

'Hasn't really changed,' he told me as though I was the *South Bank Show* crew. Both of us looked around at the road we were standing on. 'Makes Cleethorpes look prosperous, doesn't it?' he said, taking the first of many photographs. 'But going abroad wasn't even an option. We were a working-class family from Manchester. It was perfectly acceptable to go to North Wales. That's what lots of people did.'

We walked around Abergele and my dad talked some more about holidays during the 1950s and early 60s. He told me how important it was to follow the landlady's rules. She would dictate where you could play, when meals were served, and give you strict instructions. The main one was not to bring sand into the house.

'Whenever sand did find its way into the bedrooms it would be a group effort,' my dad recalled. 'We'd all get on our hands and knees and pick it up speck by speck.'

Once they even went to the trouble of buying a dustpan and brush just to sweep up the little bits of sand, being too terrified of the owner to ask if they could use hers. It was a strange dread, that if they did not behave properly they would not be allowed to return. It was only a holiday flatlet, but they obeyed the rules rigidly. It wasn't just my dad and his family who were scared of the landlady.

'The rule everyone remembers with the landladies', my dad continued, 'is once breakfast was over no-one was allowed back into the house. It didn't matter how bad the weather was, we had to be out until teatime. They really were ruthless.'

The next place my dad took me to was Talacre. I'd never heard of it before. My dad had told me it was small but even so, I was not completely expecting what I saw. There was more mud than pavement. I've been in bigger Pizza Expresses. Talacre essentially consisted of one road with an internet café and an amusement arcade. We parked up, walked through more puddles and mud in footwear not prepared for negotiating a swamp, before reaching the beach: two and half acres of the emptiest space you could imagine. It made Holkham look like Ayia Napa. I could imagine my dad's family arriving here. 'We've gone on holiday by mistake.'

'The thing I remember most vividly about this seaside is the pillbox,' my dad said. 'Because it was just after the War there were still remnants of frontline protection on the beach. We used to play with all sorts. It was probably pretty dangerous. It'll be long gone by now.'

On the beach was a lighthouse, the oldest in Wales. Built in 1777, it is Grade II listed, and had sold a few months earlier for around £90,000. Its previous owner had spent years restoring it, a personal campaign to save the lighthouse and its heritage. The lighthouse comes with many tales of sightings of ghosts, including one story, told by the Pathfinder Paranormal Investigators, that the spirit of a man called Raymond, a lighthouse man who died of a broken heart, might still be connected to the lighthouse. There is also the chance that it might not be.

Never must the loneliness of the lighthouse keeper have been more evident than in Talacre. If I was a wealthy philanthropist I'd have bought it, put a drum kit at the top and allowed local kids to come and play to their heart's content. There is no bigger luxury than being able to make a loud noise with no-one to complain. I was thinking about this, and my other philanthropic outlets, as we walked across the crinkle-cut sand, when my dad stopped in his tracks.

'It's still there,' he said, astonished.

Two little boys were playing with what looked like a lump of metal. We stood and watched for a while before my dad walked over to have a closer look.

'Do you know what this is?' my dad asked.

'No,' they said.

'I don't know either,' their mum admitted.

'It's a pillbox. A gun emplacement. It was used during the Second World War to fire machine guns.'

'Cooool!' the boys replied, their imaginations going into Hollywood overdrive as they thought of ammunition being sprayed and baddy soldiers theatrically falling on the beach. They were right. It was pretty cool.

'I used to play here when I was their age,' my dad told their mum. 'This is the first time I've been back since.'

The beach hadn't changed since then. Not even slightly. How many places in the world could you say haven't changed even remotely in such a long period of time? The tide came in. The tide went out again. But the machine-gun pillbox and the lighthouse were still there, abandoned, disused, with people reliant on someone like my dad happening to wander along and fill in pieces of social history.

'I have no idea why Talacre was so attractive to our family for so many years,' my dad continued as we walked back to the car. 'We'd always be in our swimming costumes in the sand dunes freezing to death, hiding from the wind. But remember, your grandma and her sisters were cooped up in a hot, sticky factory all year so I suppose just being outdoors was exactly what they needed. Life was just queues back then: at shops, at bus stops, at railway stations. Very few people had their own transport but everyone seemed so patient and so resilient to all obstacles that came their way. I never really remember anyone moaning. Apart from the seaside landladies.'

Llandudno, known as the Queen of the Welsh resorts as early as 1864, was the last seaside we wanted to stop off at. This seemed a much more recognisable seaside town; it wasn't as still, there weren't so many wide-open spaces. There was a promenade, a high street, a pier advertising rides on a speedboat. We went there for a wander and ended up at a café. My dad told me that when they were in Llandudno, one of the big attractions for the adults was sitting in a deckchair and having a pot of tea on the beach. There was a ten-shilling deposit, a huge amount for a ceramic teapot. But they all felt decadent sitting on the beach drinking a cup of tea.

'Remember,' he said to me as the waitress cleared away our tray, 'back then we had so little. People spent their whole lives working. A cup of tea on the beach was the height of luxury, a real treat. Back then we rarely got a cup of tea like that, it was too expensive. There are so, so many things people take for granted now.'

It was slightly strange to think that all this took place such a relatively short time ago. As it was my dad telling me about these holidays, in the same voice he used when reading out Roald Dahl or C S Lewis stories, it just seemed like it was make-believe, fantasy, or at worst an allegory. It was difficult to comprehend that all this had been just a few decades earlier; people had such a different way of life back then.

I realised how lucky I was being able to have all those childhood trips to Scarborough and Whitby, even Cleethorpes, and when we were older those fortnights in France every summer. At the time I remember being jealous of all the kids in my class at school who went to Florida, pissing about with Mickey Mouse, while we were in a B&B in Robin Hood's Bay. The ingratitude of children.

Walking back along the pier and the seafront, what really struck me were all the benches in memoriam. This was something I'd seen in every seaside town, and sometimes with the Cleethorpes boating lake and the Southwold plaques they would be done in a very tasteful and thoughtful way. But I'd never seen them quite as prominent as they seemed to be in Llandudno. There was clearly a very elderly population.

As in Eastbourne, you got the sense that the people who walked past us were also enjoying their day in Wales, simply retracing footsteps. My dad and I weren't the only people thinking about the olden days. Everything moved at Zimmer-frame speed. An old couple sat down on a bench next to where we were walking. Another bench dedicated to someone who loved Llandudno. To me it had just been a place on the map I was interested in visiting, another seaside to tick off my list. To some people, it was the whole world.

As we drove away, my dad fondly remembered the 'I can see the sea' game so familiar to all of us. He used to play it with his cousins on the way to Blackpool. All the children were offered sixpence for the first person to see Blackpool Tower. His cousin Barrie always got bored with looking. He always started when they were only a mile or so from home – he was clueless about geography. It was always my dad who spotted it. Despite the promises, he never got his sixpence.

'Sometimes there'd be a pylon alongside the railway track and Barrie would think that was the tower.' My dad shook his head, still in disbelief. 'Pylons,' he said and drove on.

CHAPTER NINETEEN

A Grand Night Out

'You're not a vegetarian, are you?' the Blackpool landlady asked as she showed me to my room.

'No.'

'Good!' she said. 'We hate it when we get vegetarians staying!'

Never before had I considered giving up meat so strongly. I'm not a vegetarian but I am on their side. I'm not against people having morals. But there I was, the only one in the dining room. Radio 4 was on as I sat down with the copy of that morning's *Mirror* provided. On the *Today* programme John Humphrys was talking about rising unemployment figures, the shrinking of the UK economy.

'Full English?' the landlady asked.

'Yes please,' I said, but was very aware I was the only person staying there. I didn't feel I was able to relax as a guest, it felt as if I had my own domestic help. When my breakfast arrived I felt bad I had paid so little for my stay: £22. I'd spend that on a good hash brown.

When I finished my fried things the landlady hovered as she collected my empty plate and she told me how quiet they had been recently. She blamed our Chancellor, gesturing at the photograph of his depressingly cheesy grin on the front page of my newspaper. Both of us knew her bed and breakfast was unlikely to survive much longer, so rapid had the rate of B&B closures been over recent years. Some businesses in Blackpool had been charging as little as £7 a night for accommodation. It did not help that dovetailing with the decline of visitors at seaside towns was the rise of the budget hotel, undercutting the costs of local accommodation with their bland but reasonably priced identical rooms. There were just too many rooms available and not enough people to sleep in the freshly made beds.

At the few bed and breakfasts in which I'd stayed in the seaside towns over the previous few months, the owners I'd met had tended to be charming, considerate proprietors, offering help, suggestions and friendly smiles. I had particularly enjoyed a couple of nights in the bed and breakfast in Scarborough I'd stayed at when working at the summer school in August. On my way there I'd had a phone call from the owner saying she'd be out when I arrived but that she'd left a key under the doormat and that I should let myself in. I felt like a teenager, whose parents have had a chat and decided I was old enough to take on new responsibilities. The comments in the guest book there had shown what a pleasant place it was to stay: 'What a lovely way to finish our honeymoon'; 'Thanks for making me feel part of the family'; 'Thank you for letting us walk your dog.'

The owner of the B&B I'd stayed at in Clacton had been equally welcoming. After my rain-soaked day and late midnight walk, it had been reassuring to be greeted with a cheery 'Hello John' the following morning. Remembering someone's name is such a small gesture but for those away from home something as simple as being greeted by your name is a refreshing burst of reassurance. I remembered, too, how the owner there had greeted an old lady walking into the breakfast room, looking around for a free table.

'Sorry mate!' he'd called out to her, gesturing at her bare feet. 'You can't come in here like that. Go and put your slippers on!'

Staying somewhere for the night hadn't always been such a pleasant experience. In the late 1800s, when holidaying first became a tradition, boarding houses started to appear at seaside resorts. These were often run by landladies who seem to have been the most despicable people in the world. As my dad had explained about North Wales, everyone who had experienced these boarding houses had harrowing memories as they recalled their days on holiday under the supervision of ladies who didn't even have first names. I don't think I'd have been able to cope.

I'd tended to be so well looked after when I had stayed in bed and breakfasts and hotels that I wondered whether they thought I was an inspector. I used to work in a hotel and we were all very aware that it was likely anyone writing a report would be travelling alone, without much luggage, staying for just the one night. Also I was quite often in the bar in the evenings with a notebook. That might explain the unusually high levels of respect I've been enjoying. I'd even been tempted to phone in advance with an anonymous tip-off that a hotel inspector was on his way and give a description of myself. That would make sure I got a comfy mattress and they didn't burn my toast.

Blackpool had come into its own as a holiday resort with the introduction of Wakes Week. This was when factory towns across the North of England shut down for a week, allowing thousands of workers to head to beach resorts across the UK. The first official Wakes Week was in 1907, and it was particularly popular after the end of the Second World War. At the start of Wakes Week in Blackburn in 1945, holidaymakers queued at the railway station from early in the morning to catch one of the 23 trains heading to Blackpool. The following Saturday, it was estimated that 250,000 people were crammed into the resort. This tradition carried on for years and it's a big reason for the development of the seaside. However, it died out as soon as we became a credit-card nation who fly around, holidaying when it pleases us. The factories are no longer in control.

Memories of Wakes Week remain strong. Interviewed in the *Lancashire Telegraph*, a lady called Margo Grimshaw recalled that, going on their Wakes Week holiday to Blackpool, her mum would treat the family to a bar of Lux scented soap. 'Well, I mean, you couldn't let the boarding-house owners know you used Fairy, could you?' In 2011, a letter in the Burnley Express recalled the stampede to get away from everyday life on the first Friday of July: *'The towns of Burnley, Nelson and Colne would all fall silent on the Friday evening as the mills would close down for the two-week break. Burnley Central Station would see extra trains (some 10 carriages long) leaving the area for an overnight journey down to the south of England, arriving there in the early hours of the next morning. Those days will never come back unfortunately but the memories will never go away. Happy days!'*

My own visit to Blackpool was to watch Paul Merton perform his new stand-up show at the Grand Theatre, the third date of his first tour for 13 years. It had been snowing on the day I booked my ticket on a bitterly cold January afternoon. It seemed strange to be at my desk looking through books about the seaside while snow was falling outside my bedroom window. I had been reading about the faded glamour of seaside theatres and wanted to see some of the venues that had survived. Blackpool has long been synonymous with comedy and entertainment, and the Grand Theatre had often played a key role.

The Grand Theatre, with its four tiers and 1,200 capacity, opened in 1894. In the pre-War years the main attraction was Gracie Fields, who appeared there between 1932 and 1938. The first summer season show was in 1940. Blackpool remained largely untouched during the War, and details have since emerged that this was because Adolf Hitler wanted the town for himself; Michael Cole, a publisher in York, found maps and aerial photographs in a military base in Germany, which suggested that Hitler had big plans for Blackpool. As a result of the lack of bomb damage, the Grand Theatre was able to continue running during the War; stars appearing there included John Gielgud, Vivien Leigh and John Mills. The holidaymakers of the 1950s and 1960s would remember the Grand for the highly successful summer season farces, starring comedy favourites like Arthur Askey, Thora Hird and Sid James.

Increasingly, though, anything outside of the summer season was tough going, and the theatre was forced to close throughout the winter. One of the reasons for this was the growth of television. More and more people were starting to stay in their living rooms, content for their cultural needs to be catered for by telly, a habit that has never disappeared. It reached the stage that by July 1972, the Tower Company, who owned the Grand Theatre, applied for permission to demolish it and build a department store instead. Luckily for theatre lovers, but less luckily for those in the North West who would have liked a nice new department store, this did not happen.

In 1994, the President of Blackpool Grand Theatre, Burt Briggs, wrote down his memories of how the Grand managed to be saved from this demolition, which have since been published on the theatre's website: 'because the Grand was by now a listed building, an enquiry was set up,' he recalled. 'An Inspector called to consider all the evidence concerning plans for its demolition. The Minister refused listed building consent for demolition of the Grand on August 15th 1973.' In 1974, a campaign called Save The Grand was put in motion, with the backing of many local businesses and firms. The campaign worked and in

September 1980 the theatre was bought by the Blackpool Grand Theatre Trust Limited.

After the purchase of the theatre, members of the Friends of the Grand helped to refurbish the dressing rooms and backstage areas in readiness for its reopening. In the week of Monday March 23 1981 Timothy West and Prunella Scales starred in the Old Vic production of *The Merchant of Venice*. The Grand seems to have been enjoying a new lease of life ever since. In 2006 Equity named it the UK's National Theatre of Variety. It enjoyed a full restoration in 2007 after a £3 million investment.

Despite only having been there once before, and that was when I was about six to see the bloody illuminations, I have always been intrigued by Blackpool. Paul Merton seemed the ideal person to see perform there. For some their introduction to comedy was Monty Python or Spike Milligan or *The Young Ones*, but for me it was Paul Merton's Channel 4 series in the early 1990s, which is why I thought this would be the perfect opportunity to check out such a special town for myself.

Blackpool is closely associated with comedy and entertainment. The George Formby convention is held every year at the Imperial Hotel; his song *Blackpool Rock (With My Little Stick Of)* was banned by the BBC because of its suggestive lyrics. It was on the North Pier, meanwhile, that Harry Corbett saw a yellow glove puppet for sale when he was on holiday with his family in 1948. That yellow bear, originally called Teddy, had its name changed to Sooty, with his catchphrase 'Izzy wizzy, let's get busy'.

Blackpool is also where Eric Morecambe and Ernie Wise met in 1939, and as a result comedy was never the same again. They first appeared on stage in Blackpool at the Winter Gardens in 1953. They continued to perform regularly at venues all across town and did their final turn there in 1965 at the ABC Theatre. At the same venue in that same year, the Beatles performed *Yesterday*, the first time it was ever seen on television, on a show called *Blackpool Night Out*. The rest of The Beatles left the stage while Paul played it on his own, after which John Lennon joined him on stage with the words, 'Thank you Ringo, that was wonderful.' Then all four of them closed the show with 'our latest record', *Help!*

A year after the second and final season of *Blackpool Night Out* ended, there was a new programme on television to distract people from going to actual theatres. This was *The Blackpool Show*, presented by Tony Hancock, running from 1966 to 1967, and it was appearing on this show that helped propel Les Dawson to fame. Others to have appeared on *The Blackpool Show* included Matt Monro, Arthur Askey, Frankie Howerd, Lenny the Lion, Roy Castle and Bob Monkhouse. This is one of the reasons why Blackpool was so synonymous with comedy – it was regularly being pumped into people's living rooms, and suddenly the whole of the UK was aware that Blackpool was somewhere special for comedy.

Another regular visitor to Blackpool was Tommy Cooper, performing at both the Pavilion Pier and the Winter Gardens. Cooper was a regular visitor to seaside resorts; his shows at Bournemouth Winter Gardens broke all box-office records, as did his shows in Scarborough, and he still made regular appearances at Skegness, even when his schedule was hectic with so much television work. Tony Hancock was also a regular performer in Blackpool, performing at theatres in 1949, 1950, 1951 and 1954. A *Spectator* article in 2011 explained that for comedians, 'Blackpool used to be the top ticket, final confirmation that you'd really made it'.

As someone born in 1981, it has always excited me that there would have been a time there a new Beatles album was about to be released. The footage of John, Paul, George and the other one messing around on stage, the most famous band in the world at a time when they were clearly enjoying performing more than ever, is preserved on YouTube. During the closing credits, The Beatles were joined by other acts on the show that night: Lionel Blair and Mike and Bernie Winters joined a line of dancing girls, entertaining the audience, both in Blackpool and in their living rooms, all of them saying, 'We are young and it's 1965 – life will not ever get better than this for anyone.'

It could not last. The ABC Theatre later became a cinema and then Syndicate Nightclub: *a Mecca for all things PARTY! Celebrating a Birthday, Anniversary, Wedding, Divorce, Stag Do, Hen Do, Agadoo! We don't care!! Get on your fancy dress, your glad rags, put your slap on and get to THE Biggest and ONLY place to PARTY in Blackpool.* What was once the centre of variety went on to be the venue with the largest revolving dance floor in Europe. In 2011 it was announced on the nightclub's Facebook page that trading was to cease, and the club is now closed, the building threatened with demolition.

A campaign soon took shape to fight plans to turn such a rich, historic venue into a car park.

This is why I had needed to come to Blackpool. It wasn't just to see a comedy gig: it genuinely felt like if I didn't go to the Grand there and then, if I left it another year or so, it would be a Wetherspoon's pub or a Tesco Metro. Just as I had experienced in Redcar and Brighton, Blackpool had a very clearly defined plan to survive the recession and the lack of holidaymakers. A large part of this involved drunk girls in wedding veils wearing L plates, most likely being pestered by groups of lads with gel in their hair.

I ordered a drink and looked around the theatre. There was a plaque commemorating the visit of Queen Elizabeth and her mate Philip, who visited the theatre in 1994 to celebrate the Grand's centenary. I sat in the bar before the show. This was a place of traditions; men with pints of beer, ladies with their something-and-tonics. It felt like a real event to be in a building with a nice carpet, chandeliers, waitresses in uniforms and well-turned-out folk chatting. The 'Let's go and do stuff' people. On the next table a group of four discussed their ideal *Just a Minute* panel. Standing next to the bar, a man announced to his colleagues, 'I met Murray Walker once.'

Blackpool Grand Theatre was Les Dawson's favourite venue. Dawson lived not far away, in Lytham St Anne's, and he starred at the theatre in the 1984 summer season show,

Laugh With Les, with the Roly Polys. He returned in 1986 with the play *Run For Your Wife*. These days, the upcoming shows at Blackpool Grand Theatre are pretty diverse: when I visited they included the Alan Bennett play *The Lady in the Van*, Roy 'Chubby' Brown, and *The Diary of Anne Frank* with Christopher Timothy. Later in the year the pantomime boasted guest star 'Aaron from *Emmerdale*'.

A lady from the Friends of the Grand asked me if I want to buy a lapel badge for £1 to help contribute to the funding of the theatre. 'That'll go through the washing machine by mistake,' I said to myself as I pinned it to my shirt. Soon it was time to go to my seat in the stalls. I was excited. Paul Merton was one of my guys and his performance was every bit in keeping with the legendary names who had appeared in the theatre and town decades and decades before.

After the show, the Grand Theatre emptied pretty quickly. Where there had been a few thousand people, now there was just me and a barman, who poured me a pint while I savoured the moment of the post-show and the surroundings. It was just the two of us for half an hour or so. I felt like I should have been drinking scotch and ice. Outside there were a few people waiting by the stage door hoping to get Paul Merton to autograph something.

'You should check out the Comedy Carpet,' the barman told me. He said the 2,000-metre-square engraving unveiled by Ken Dodd in 2011 was a must for all comedy fans. I had been asking about the posters in the foyer. Jimmy Logan in *Loganberry Pie*. Gilbert and Sullivan operas. *A Taste of Honey*. It was an era I was fascinated by. I loved talk of old comedy. There's nothing I like more than to watch old Laurel and

Hardies or *Hancock's Half Hour*, I immerse myself in the worlds they created. Everything about Blackpool seemed to fit well with me.

I wasn't in the mood to go straight back to my B&B. It just didn't seem right. A walk along Blackpool seafront late at night seemed the only suitable way to end the night. During his show, Paul Merton had talked about the importance of stories, of imagination, and that stayed with me as I walked away from the theatre and out across the promenade, enjoying Blackpool on a warm evening, thinking about the importance of comedy both for me and for the seaside.

The next morning I took the barman's advice and went for a wander to find the Comedy Carpet. It was on the promenade between Blackpool Tower and the beach and involved 300 granite slabs, and listed names of more than 1,000 comedians, from Max Bygraves to Russell Brand, Bob Carolgees and Spit the Dog to Peter Cook.

It was a sunny morning and there were perhaps 20 of us admiring the artwork by Gordon Young, 'a visual artist who focuses on creating art for the public domain'. He was also responsible for the typography on the pavements at the much-loved Eric Morecambe statue on Morecambe seafront, which was where I planned to visit next.

The common denominator for all Young's projects was the relevance of the surroundings. This looked like a fun project to be part of. I stooped down to read complete sketches engraved on the floor; song lyrics, dialogue between artists such as The Two Ronnies, Eric and Ernie, French and Saunders. A lady sang the lyrics to Monty Python's *Spam* song to her son in a pushchair, who laughed uncontrollably at what must have been his first taste of Monty Python and the repetition of spam, spam, spam. There were catchphrases on the carpet: *Suit You, Sir, Oh, Miss Jones, You stupid boy*. I read memorable lines by everyone from Stan and Ollie to *The Office*. Comedy was everywhere.

In the largest letters of all, each specially measured so they could be seen from the top of the Blackpool Tower, was the Bruce Forsyth slogan, *Nice to see you, to see you nice*. It was not just the names of the greats – Frankie Howerd, Les Dawson, Tommy Cooper – there are also contemporary comedians mentioned, such as Laura Solon and Jack Whitehall.

The quotations were well chosen, and the most impressive thing about the Comedy Carpet was the lack of ostentation. It was there to make people happy, public art at its best, a folk history, so many memories on each paving stone. Which is why later I was so alarmed to read that contractors from Blackpool Council had destroyed parts of the artwork because of fears it was too close to the tram tracks.

At first when I read that some of the Comedy Carpet had been destroyed, I assumed it would have been due to graffiti. If anything, this discovery was even worse; knowing it had all been authorised made it almost unforgivable. Gordon Young was distraught. The Council has ripped up five of his slabs nearest the tram track, fearing visitors might step backwards under a tram while reading them. The five slabs contained the names of 100 comedians. Council workmen had trimmed the stones, damaging them in the process of removing them.

'I cannot believe the Council has done this,' Young was reported to have said in the *Guardian*. 'Not only have they ruined my artwork and removed the names of so many comedians whose work I wanted to celebrate, but they have even destroyed the dedication stone.' This occurred within six months of Ken Dodd opening it, a news story receiving much acclaim at the time from broadsheets and comedy lovers everywhere.

'It was a huge honour to have Ken Dodd unveil the Comedy Carpet,' Young said. 'I am gobsmacked that the Council should treat him so shabbily.' When the news was announced, he and his collaborator, Andy Altman, were about to travel to Japan to collect the prestigious Tokyo Grand Prix design award, beating competition from over 3,200 projects from all across the globe. I had come to Blackpool to see the faded glamour of the seaside, theatres and comedy. It seemed the Council was happy to oblige with a visual representation of this.

That, though, was for the future. On the weekend of my visit, the sun shone and people were enjoying the artwork. Each punchline and name on the ground evoked a different memory: all of us were walking around replaying videotapes of our childhoods in our minds. The lady had stopped singing the *Spam* song, and was, rather gratifyingly, explaining to her son who Trevor and Simon were. The highlight for us were the parts of the Carpet devoted to Morecambe and Wise. It was time to go somewhere I had read about often, but never visited: the Eric Morecambe statue on Morecambe seafront.

CHAPTER TWENTY

Looking for Eric

The final visit of my tour of British seaside towns was to the Lancashire resort of Morecambe. As I took the train from Blackpool, the man opposite me was reading the *Sunday Mail*, whose headline boasted 'Coats off as temperatures reach record high.' We were enjoying hotter weather than Athens, Rome and Barcelona. Every front cover of every glossy magazine at the newsagent by the station had contained the summer's diet tips; everyone was being told to think of their tummies once more – 'God, I wish I looked like Cheryl on this beautiful sunny day.' Everywhere I looked there were sunbathers; there wasn't a patch of grass which didn't have sprawled teenagers who should have been revising, using textbooks for pillows.

As we travelled north, it seemed that on each train platform people were lying down, enjoying the few minutes in the sun before their train arrived. Time had suddenly taken on a new meaning; the announcement of a delay was welcome – all of a sudden, it meant a few more rare, cherished moments in the unbroken sunshine.

After so many days spent shivering in out-of-season seaside towns I felt I deserved this piece of sun. There was so much to love about this time of year: flowery maxi-dresses everywhere, lads with their tops off, people adjusting their brand-new sunglasses, in which you could see the reflection of others adjusting their brand-new sunglasses. People were wearing three-quarter-length trousers and sandals, bare legs were visible once more. This is what it was like on the train from Blackpool, people cheerful for the first time since Christmas morning. Across the country there would have been hundreds of thousands of people doing the same, in trains and in hot, sweaty cars heading to seaside towns, looking for somewhere to park. I looked around my carriage; we were all wearing our smiles like expensive trainers. We were going to the seaside.

Morecambe was where Alan Bennett went on holiday as a child. In his diaries he revealed that August Bank Holiday at the seaside was when he was conceived, as was his older brother, who shared the same May birthday.

The town, more famously, was loved by Eric Morecambe. That is generally the case if you choose a town to use as your stage name. Perhaps it is more accurate to say that Morecambe was so important to Eric Bartholmew. Eric's dad worked on a market stall in Morecambe. Both Eric's parents were buried in the town. Eric's first child Gail was born in Morecambe while Eric was on summer season in Blackpool.

I walked up to the statue. He's on one leg, one hand in the air, in his familiar pose, and he's never looked happier. I had to wait for a moment for the people having their photograph taken to leave and walk off down the seafront, because I felt I wanted to be alone with the statue. I looked down at the etched lyrics. Rarely are the lines of a song so perfect and pertinent to our way of life as the lyrics to *Bring Me Sunshine*.

The statue had been unveiled by the Queen and the Duke of Edinburgh, who I think might also be writing a book about the seaside: they have visited everywhere I've been over the last few months. I'm starting to get worried, I'm not sure I'll be able to compete with the PR engine over at Buckingham Palace. The Queen, taking time out of her busy career writing non-fiction books, told the President of the Eric Morecambe Fan Club, David Miles, that both she and the Duke of Edinburgh were great fans of the double act.

At the ceremony, the Royal couple were joined by Eric's widow, Joan Bartholomew, and their children Gail, Gary and Steven. Also invited to the statue's unveiling were guests who had worked with the comedy pair during *The Morecambe and Wise Show*'s television heyday, including the legendary broadcaster Sir Robin Day. Day explained to the BBC that Morecambe was 'a genius, a genius in his sphere, like Einstein or Beethoven. A genius of his art of making people happy. I was on the show several times, notably when I was hit over the head with a bottle. I wouldn't have missed this for the world.'

The area around the statue contained numerous catchphrases plus the names of each one of the 103 special guests who had appeared on *The Morecambe and Wise Show*. I stood there in the sunshine reading each carefully crafted letter, but more than that I was looking at my fellow Eric Morecambe pilgrims. Everyone was smiling. It was a beautiful thing to see. YouTube is full of videos of people's own trips to the statue; dancing, posing with Eric. It's the same if you look for it on Google Images. It is a compendium of happiness and simplicity.

It hasn't always been so happy and sunny for Morecambe in recent years. In fact, the town had been through some grim times. The Winter Gardens, which were once managed by Thora Hird's father, have been closed since 1977, the year The Sex Pistols performed in Cleethorpes. The Grade II listed building was built in 1870 and included a ballroom, seawater baths and bars.

The Friends of the Winter Gardens formed in 1986, a group of local residents who shared the same strong feelings and concerns for the building. 'At the start, our prime role was to keep up pressure to save the theatre from demolition,' a spokesperson for the group explained on their website. 'During this time, we went into the Pavilion enthusiastically with mops and buckets to clean up this once beautiful building and, to give back some of its lost sparkle, we cleaned away years of dirt and rubbish.'

The Friends of the Winter Gardens now own the building. They made a film with the BBC, which is genuinely moving: the contrast of past and present is breathtaking. 'Last October we had the lead stolen from our roof,' Evelyn Archer, Chairman of the Friends of the Winter Gardens, told the BBC. 'We put in a claim to our insurers and they still haven't settled it. Over the last few days we've had torrential rain. How could we afford to re-create a building like this?'

Watching the film online, the era bursts out of the computer screen. gold gilding, the figures over the proscenium, people waltzing in the dance hall who had spent the afternoon swimming in the lido. Visiting performers to the Winter Gardens have included Elgar, Shirley Bassey, Tommy Steele and, of course, Morecambe and Wise. 'It's been a place of entertainment,' Evelyn said. 'Days of laughter. Of people enjoying themselves.'

As if to demonstrate the contrast of old-day spectacular theatre and modern-day pop culture blandness, the Morecambe MP David Morris tabled a Commons Motion to save the Winter Gardens, citing the support of *Baywatch* actor David Hasselhoff as a key reason. Morris claimed the actor's endorsement 'demonstrates the international significance of the Winter Gardens'. It also demonstrated that they were clutching at straws, running out of ideas on what to do next.

As well as the uncertainty over the Winter Gardens, Morecambe had also not been helped by the disaster which was Blobbyland: the theme park inspired by *Noel's House Party's* much-loved resident, Mr Blobby (although it now seems hard to believe that was ever the case). The Crinkly

Bottom theme park in Morecambe closed just 13 weeks after it was opened in 1994. The ensuing legal battle cost the council £2.5 million.

Although it's one of those news stories easy to laugh at, the damage to Morecambe was considerable. The seaside town was already going through a strange time. Fashion designer Wayne Hemingway recalled happy times as a boy in Morecambe: 'Growing up in a kitsch town like Morecambe, I was surrounded by knitted poodle toilet-roll holders, little felt bulls, donkeys, sherry decanters, things people brought back from holiday. It's given me a sense of humour.'

Hemingway, one of the patrons of the Morecambe Winter Gardens, found the town had become run-down in later years: 'In the years since I left Morecambe and especially in the years living in the South, every time I went back the seafront became more and more unloved.' Council leader Ian Barker admitted: 'I think Morecambe became briefly a laughing stock.' He felt compelled to utter a sentence I'm sure he'd never have expected to use in his council career. 'We must learn the lessons of Crinkly Bottom.' The incident was dubbed 'Blobbygate' in *The Independent*.

The Council began legal action, blaming the failure on the pre-*Deal or No Deal* Noel Edmonds' lack of interest. They even blamed Mr Blobby for 'his lack of corpulence', accusing Noel Edmonds of supplying an underweight Mr Blobby to the theme park.

Urban Realm magazine, continuing the ridiculous theme, explained that the big problem with Blobbygate was that 'the expected tourists never turned up, meaning a surplus of bed and breakfasts, meaning Morecambe became a bit of a dumping ground for "problem folk", a familiar tale for many British seaside towns.'

The Eric Morecambe statue, by contrast, had given the whole town a lift. I realised this was what I had been looking for when I'd been going from seaside to seaside. I have been looking for Eric. The film *Looking for Eric* could easily have applied to Morecambe rather than Cantona. Ken Loach's film is about an ageing postman who hallucinates the presence of Eric Cantona, the footballer he once worshipped on the terraces at Old Trafford, to help guide him through his increasingly difficult life. This is what people seemed to be doing with Eric Morecambe.

Standing next to the statue, posing for the compulsory photograph, I felt as if Eric was going to put both hands on my shoulders then slap my cheeks, in the way he so often did to Ernie Wise. This was somewhere to gather for like-minded people. In this world where we live, there should be more happiness.

People can't get enough of Eric Morecambe. If Morecambe seafront had 100 statues of Eric Morecambe there wouldn't have been a single complaint; each one of them would have people being photographed beside it. A thousand Eric Morecambe statues would just pose the question that maybe there should be 1,000 more Eric Morecambe statues, the number of Eric statues increasing exponentially over the next few years.

The statue has given the town its signature, its main attraction. A 1992 article in *The Independent* had feared for the town's future at a time when neighbouring Blackpool was flourishing. Looking across the bay to the hills of the Lake District, it has been described as 'more failed than any comparable resort in the country'. But the statue seems to have gone a long way to making everything better. There was still deprivation, Morecambe still had its social problems, as do so many small towns, coastal or otherwise. But in a world of faded glamour, some things will glisten forever.

Epilogue

I spent the next day in Morecambe having a genuine holiday: no writing, no teaching, no meetings. Just sitting on the beach, reading, exploring with no specific purpose. The things you're supposed to do at the seaside.

It was strange to think that all the time I'd been travelling around, every single day there were people at sea in their lifeboats. Ross and his team were patrolling Beachy Head. The man on his ferry was taking people across the water to Flushing. James was showing people around the saucy postcard museum. There were people on the Walk the Dog simulator on the pier, or at their kitchen tables writing letters to local MPs and newspapers campaigning to restore parts of their town, trying to reconnect to the past.

I'd lost count of the number of times I had slipped on seaweed while walking over rocks. Stopped in my tracks watching the building of a sandcastle: the moment the upturned bucket was lifted to determine success or failure. I'd played on so many 2p machines in amusement arcades, eaten so many cones of chips. Most of all I'd been moved by so many plaques. All the benches in memoriam.

I had seen the sun at every gradient in the sky, walked on more sand than pavement, and spent far too much time gazing at people, wondering about their lives, watching how they behaved. I hadn't realised there would be so much to learn, not just about the people but the places, the history, the future. Who would have thought that even somewhere like Cleethorpes would have had so much romance to it?

When I first started working at the summer school in Scarborough, my feelings about the seaside were pretty similar to most people's. I liked seaside resorts, had always enjoyed them, but didn't know a huge amount about their development or historical significance. I had assumed that they were all pretty much the same: a beach, some shops, a man hiring out deckchairs, perhaps a pier. But after talking to so many people who devoted their lives to seasides, who lived there, had grown up there, worked there, I quickly became fascinated.

I had found out that the seaside isn't just a thing of the past; these towns and resorts exist, and hopefully will always be loved and cared for. It was Gerry talking about automation and Steve the Cleethorpes journalist reliving his nostalgia through YouTube that made me realise we had to move with the times. Ryanair exists. Laurel and Hardy don't. This was the world we lived in now.

My journey had given me time to reflect, to visit the places I was familiar with from growing up, see in real life all the photographs in the albums at my mum and dad's house, with the dates written on the back. To remember all those journeys to the seaside, me and my sister asleep in the back.

Not long after returning from Morecambe, I found myself back at Southwold Pier. I looked across the beach at the kids playing, chasing one another around, running into the sea. One day, I thought, they will look back at this fondly.

The reason I had come back was because over the previous few months I had been so taken by those commemorative plaques. I hadn't been able to get them out of my head. I was moved by the tiny dedications: the proposals, birthdays and to-the-dearly-departeds, snapshots of people's lives in a sentence. I wanted to come back and look at them again. I don't know if it was because of the amount of time I'd spent at the seaside over the previous months, the amount I'd read and heard about romance and pride and families and traditions. I found it almost too much to read them for more than a few minutes at a time. But it made me happy, too. I now knew that when things get bad I could always come to Southwold Pier. Or if I did move away somewhere new, the first thing I would do would be to check to the local beaches.

I looked at the different family mottos on the plaques on the pier: *'First to see the lighthouse, ten pence', The Gould family; Look out for the Staceys! Four generations and beyond!; 'Oh no not again!' The Berridge family.* They got to me every time. Most of all it was the simplicity. These were people's lives, and people, generally, were happy.

I think I've always known that about my own family, but this last year visiting the seaside had really proved how lucky I was: not just to have been on so many holidays, but also to have been able to appreciate them, to have such fond memories. Which is why, if you visit Southwold Pier and look hard enough, you will see another plaque, with the words:

The Osbornes
who love the seaside.
Mum and Dad
Karen and John.

Acknowledgements

I would like to express warmth and gratitude to all the people who helped me with the writing of this book, the people I met and spoke to over the phone and who have told me their seaside stories: Chris Baron, Carl Chapple, Rebecca Crooks, Tamsin Curry, Wayne Hemingway, Tim Hunkin, Steve Jackson, Lisa Heledd Jones, Kenneth Marshall, Gerry Douglas-Sherwood, James Bissell-Thomas, Rebecca Worth.

Thanks to Brigitte Aphrodite, Gaz and everyone at Latham's Brasserie in Hastings. All the Mr Punches. Ross, Ben, Nicola and all the volunteers on the Beachy Head Chaplaincy Team.

Thanks to Jane Berthoud, Helen Brocklehurst, Tom Bromley, Mike Jones, Henry Layte and the Book Hive in Norwich and, as always, Rebecca Winfield.

Thanks to all the positive, helpful, encouraging people I am surrounded by: Katie Bonna, Laura Calnan, Tim Clare, Suz Close, Mike, Rachel and Sophie Cole, Joe Dunthorne, Chris Gomm, Bryony Kimmings, Vikki Mizon, Tom Searle, Ross Sutherland, Dan Walker, Hannah Walker, Luke Wright.

Thanks to Patrick Lappin, although, coming from Shropshire, Britain's largest landlocked county, he will have little or no comprehension of anything included in this book.

Special thanks to Yanny Mac and Molly Naylor for driving me around and telling me their stories about the seaside.

Lastly, thanks and love to my mum, dad and my sister.